# Pearson
# Revise

T0351597

# AQA GCSE (9–1)
# History

## America, 1920–1973: Opportunity and Inequality

## Revision Guide and Workbook

Series Consultant: Harry Smith

Author: Sally Clifford

## Also available to support your revision:

Revise GCSE Study Skills Guide          9781292318875

The **Revise GCSE Study Skills Guide** is full of tried-and-trusted hints and tips for how to learn more effectively. It gives you techniques to help you achieve your best – throughout your GCSE studies and beyond!

Revise GCSE Revision Planner          9781292318868

The **Revise GCSE Revision Planner** helps you to plan and organise your time, step-by-step, throughout your GCSE revision. Use this book and wall chart to mastermind your revision.

For the full range of Pearson revision titles across KS2, 11+, KS3, GCSE, Functional Skills, AS/A Level and BTEC visit:
www.pearsonschools.co.uk/revise

# Contents

### A small bit of small print

AQA publishes Sample Assessment Material and the Specification on its website. This is the official content and this book should be used in conjunction with it. The questions and revision tasks in this book have been written to help you revise the skills you may need for your assessment. Remember: the real assessment may not look like this.

# The American people

This period study focuses on the changes that took place between 1920 and 1973, and on the impact these changes had on the American people. So it is useful to understand who the American people were.

## A British colony

- In the 1600s, British settlers set up 13 colonies along the east coast of America. The settlers established plantations and grew cotton and tobacco.

- By the late 18th century, the colonists began to resent the way Britain ruled them – taxing them and making laws but refusing to allow them representation in parliament.

- On 4 July 1776, the 13 colonies declared independence from Britain and joined together to form the United States of America.

## A new nation

The new American government drew up a constitution (set of rules) which laid down how the country should be run:

- a state government for local affairs

- a second level of government – an overarching federal government – for matters involving all states, led by a president elected every four years

- a Bill of Rights guaranteeing everyone key freedoms, such as freedom of speech and worship, access to the law, the right to own weapons and the right to access information.

## Who were the American people?

By the 1920s, the opportunity for a new life had been attracting people to America from all over the world for nearly 300 years. The 'American' population of around 110 million was, in fact, made up of over 100 different nationalities. America is often described as a 'melting pot' – this compares a multi-cultural society to a pot where different metals are melted together to form a new material.

**Recent immigrants:**
From the mid-19th century, more immigrants came to America. Some were Mexicans and Cubans looking for work, others were Jews fleeing persecution in Eastern Europe, or people escaping poverty in Italy and Greece. About a million Irish people emigrated to America as a result of the Irish Potato Famine (1845–49). There were also immigrants from China and Japan. Many of these immigrants were poor and low-skilled, and settled in large towns and cities where they tried to find work.

**African Americans:**
Millions of slaves were brought from Africa to work on the plantations in the colonies between 1600 and 1860. Slavery officially ended in 1865 and the slaves were free but they still faced huge discrimination. They could not vote, had little access to education, and had only low-paid jobs and low-quality housing. By 1920 there were about 10 million African Americans in the USA, mostly in the South.

**The 'melting pot'**

**Native Americans:**
Before the arrival of European settlers, there were tribes of native people who had lived across America for thousands of years. Over time the white settlers forced Native Americans off their land and made them live in small 'reservations'. This had a huge impact on the native population, which dropped to just 5% of its original level in less than 300 years.

**Descendants of early settlers:**
From the 1600s onwards, white settlers came to America from Europe – mainly Britain, Germany and the Netherlands. These groups became the richest and most powerful people in America. From the 1960s they were often known as WASPs (White Anglo-Saxon Protestants). People from this group formed the bulk of the government well into the 20th century.

## Now try this

Suggest **two** challenges that might come from a 'melting pot' of different groups.

# Causes of the boom

A period of low unemployment, high wages and high sales is called an 'economic boom'. 1920s America was booming – many people benefited from an improved standard of living.

## The First World War

- When war broke out in 1914, the US government did not get involved. Instead, American banks lent money to Britain and its allies to buy food and weapons – mostly from America. This created a lot of jobs and wealth.

- The USA joined the war in 1917, but it was not as badly affected as its European allies. The war also damaged some of Germany's key industries, allowing America to overtake them and become the biggest producers of chemicals such as medicines and dyes.

## Consumer society

- By 1920, America was producing 70% of the world's petrol, 40% of its iron, 50% of its timber and 55% of its cotton. Access to this amount of raw materials meant that more 'consumer goods' like cars and household gadgets could be produced.

- Nearly 70% of American homes had electricity by 1929 – up from 15% in 1916. This increased demand for new inventions like radios, fridges, washing machines and cars, which created manufacturing jobs.

## Advertising and hire purchase

- The growing demand for consumer goods was increased by widespread advertising campaigns in newspapers and on billboards, as well as on the radio and in cinemas. People who lived a long way from the shops could see what was available in catalogues.

- Another development was **hire purchase** (a credit agreement where goods could be paid for in instalments). In the 1920s, 60% of cars were bought in this way.

## Industry and mass production

- American businesses took advantage of new ways of manufacturing goods.

- One of the key changes was the introduction of the **assembly line** – instead of workers making a whole product, each stage of the process was done by a different person.

- This made production much faster and allowed goods to be sold at cheaper prices.

For more about mass production, turn to page 3.

## Republican government policies

- Generally, the Republican government believed in **laissez-faire** (minimum interference) and wanted to let businesses operate without rules and restrictions. They did not regulate the stock market, which contributed to the **stock market boom**.

- Many Republicans believed in 'rugged individualism' – that people should look after their own needs and support others, not rely on the government.

- However, the Republican government did act to support American businesses, for example by cutting taxes, and by introducing **tariffs** (taxes on imported goods).

The 1922 Fordney–McCumber **Tariff Act** imposed high taxes on a wide variety of imported goods. This made American goods cheaper.

## Cycle of prosperity

Mass production leads to cheaper goods.

Consumer goods are more affordable.

People take out hire purchase to buy more goods.

Advertising causes even more demand.

More people are employed making the goods.

More jobs means less competition for jobs and wages rise.

People have more **disposable income** (money left over after essentials).

Low unemployment, high wages and high sales led to increased wealth. This meant more demand for goods, which raised profits.

**Now try this**

Explain **three** ways in which ordinary people's lives were affected by the growth of the consumer society in the 1920s.

# Ford and the motor industry

During the 1920s, Henry Ford was one of the richest men in the world, making the equivalent of £2 million a day. He did this by adopting a method called 'mass production' to make his car factories more efficient. This method quickly spread to other industries.

### Henry Ford (1863–1947)

- Ford came from a farming family. His parents were immigrants from Ireland and Belgium. He did not like farm work and in 1879 he left to become an apprentice machine operator in Detroit, Michigan.
- He founded the Ford Motor company in June 1903. His first car was the Model A, and by October he had made a profit of $37 000 – the equivalent of about $3 million today.
- He introduced the system of **mass production,** which revolutionised industry in the USA.
- He paid his workers nearly three times as much as other factory owners. This meant he attracted skilled mechanics, reducing training costs. It also meant that his employees could afford his cars!

## Mass production and the Model T

- In 1911, Ford introduced the assembly line (previously used in food packing plants) to car-making. Rather than workers building a car from start to finish, the car moved on a conveyor past workers who were each responsible for a small part of the process.

- The Ford Company concentrated on mass-producing a single type of car – the Model T. It was quick and cheap to build because they were all the same, and one colour (so they didn't have to spend time changing the paint in the spray guns).

The Ford Model T was available in black only. Black was chosen because black paint dried fastest!

- Faster production meant lower costs and cheaper cars – between 1911 and 1928 the cost of a car fell from $800 to $295. Mass production was soon adopted in other industries, which increased production and reduced prices, which further increased the boom.

The car industry created jobs – 500 000 people worked in car plants by the mid-1920s. In addition, factories making glass, tyres, leather and steel employed millions more.

By 1926 there were 20 million cars in America – this led to congestion on the roads.

Increased car use led to pollution.

### The impact of the motor industry

Cars were new and many people were not very good drivers – car accidents were frequent.

City suburbs grew because people could drive to work and no longer needed to live near their place of work.

Cars brought a sense of increased freedom and independence and also increased trade for roadside businesses like restaurants and hotels.

Mass production was widely adopted and soon everything from fridges to weapons was made on assembly lines. However, the spread of the motor car was mass production's biggest impact.

## Now try this

Write a paragraph to explain the impact mass production in the motor industry had on the economy. Give at least **two** examples in your answer.

# Inequalities of wealth

The boom created a great deal of wealth in 1920s America, but it didn't get shared around equally. There were groups who didn't benefit at all.

## Growing inequalities

- The 1920s saw a growing number of millionaires in the USA – 15 000 by 1927 – but there were also 6 million families living on less than $1000 a year. This was about 42% of the population.

- This was partly because there were lots of people who were looking for work in factories, so large firms were able to keep wages for unskilled workers low. This made the companies more profitable.

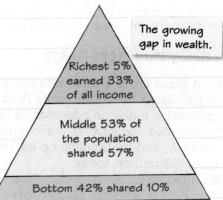

The growing gap in wealth.

Richest 5% earned 33% of all income

Middle 53% of the population shared 57%

Bottom 42% shared 10%

## Farmers

- American farmers had benefited from the First World War – European countries had imported American food because they couldn't produce their own. By the 1920s, Europe was recovering and demand for American goods was falling. Some companies added tariffs to American food prices, making them more expensive.

- New machinery meant that American farmers were making a lot more food – more than they could sell. Many had taken loans to buy the machinery and couldn't repay them, leading to eviction. In 1924 alone, more than half a million farmers lost their farms – and their labourers lost their jobs.

## The impact of new industries

- ✓ New products created jobs and wealth, but they also caused a drop in demand for traditional products.

- ✓ Skilled workers in these industries found that their skills were no longer needed, and they had to take unskilled, lower-paid work.

- ✓ The growing use of oil and petrol for cars, gas and – especially – electricity meant that demand for coal dropped, leading to the closure of coal mines.

- ✓ New synthetic fabrics like nylon pushed down the demand for cotton and wool, and workers in those industries saw their wages fall or their jobs disappear completely.

## African Americans

- Most African Americans lived in the southern states. They worked as farm labourers or rented small farms as **sharecroppers** (farmers who have to give a share of their crop to their landlord).

- Most African Americans were living in extreme poverty and their living conditions were awful. The problems that hit the farming industry hit the sharecroppers especially hard.

For more about the experiences of African Americans, see page 12.

## Native Americans

- The native people had lost most of their land as it had been seized by mining and ranching companies.

- Native Americans were forced to live on reservations. The reservations were often on the worst land where it was difficult to grow crops. They also made it harder for Native Americans to follow their traditional way of life.

- Most Native Americans lived in extreme poverty, and had lower-quality education. They had a shorter life expectancy than any other ethnic group in the USA.

## Now try this

Write a paragraph explaining why some groups of people did not benefit from the boom in the 1920s.

# The stock market boom

One of the main ways that people made money during the boom was by buying and selling shares.

## How did the stock market work?

During the 1920s, lots of people started businesses. Starting a business takes money – for example, for wages, materials and land. Some of these business people were rich enough to use their own money, but others needed to borrow.

America's stock exchange is in New York.

Investors lend money to a business. In return, the investors own a share of the business. These investors are called **shareholders** and they are paid a **dividend** (a share of the profits) every year.

If a company does well and makes large profits, it becomes worth more. This means that the shares become more valuable. Shareholders can make money by selling shares for more than they have paid for them.

During the 1920s American companies earned record profits. Most companies invested their profits in further expansion. This made share prices rise.

Shares (also called stocks) are bought and sold in the **stock market** at a **stock exchange**.

## A booming stock market

Buying shares became hugely popular during the 1920s. Stock prices were rising and rising, so it wasn't just the rich who got involved – millions of ordinary Americans bought shares too, hoping to make money from rising share values.

Lots of these people used borrowed money to buy shares, or paid a 10% deposit, hoping to pay back the loan when the shares were sold for a profit. This was called **buying on the margin** and was a good (but risky) way to make money – as long as the price of shares kept rising.

**1** The American presidents during the boom – Warren G. Harding (1921–23), Calvin Coolidge (1923–29) and Herbert Hoover (1929–33) – were Republican, and believed in laissez-faire – that the government should not interfere in the running of the economy, leaving it to businesses to create wealth.

**2** The government helped by keeping taxes as low as possible. This allowed businesses to invest more in expansion, and gave ordinary people more money to spend.

### Government policies

**3** The government also tried to help economic growth by making it easier to borrow money.

**4** The government banks relaxed the rules for credit. The American public took out loans totalling $4 billion. Some of this money was invested in shares.

## Controlling the stock market

The government's laissez-faire approach also meant that there were hardly any controls. Anyone could set up a company and sell shares. Some companies did not actually produce anything, they just bought and sold shares. This meant that the shares were not attached to anything with a fixed value. Some companies didn't actually exist at all. But while prices were rising, it didn't matter, so the government made no attempt to regulate (make rules for) the stock market.

### Now try this

Give **one** example of possible problems with the stock market.

# Entertainment

During the economic boom of the 1920s, many people had more money and leisure time. They looked for ways to enjoy themselves. This led to social and cultural changes, and the 1920s became known as the 'Roaring Twenties'.

The 1920s saw a boom in the film industry. Cinema was already popular, but audiences tripled during this period.

The movie business was based in Hollywood, outside Los Angeles on the West Coast. This area had good weather all year, which made it ideal for producing films. By the end of the decade, Hollywood studios were producing more than 500 films a year.

**The growth of cinema**

The growing popularity of cinema caused some concerns. Campaigners worried that the sexual content of some films would damage young people's morals. There were moves to ban certain films in several states. The industry responded by introducing the Hays Code, which banned screen kisses lasting more than three seconds and ensured that no character benefited from criminal behaviour.

Before 1927, films were silent. Captions appeared at regular intervals, and a pianist played music to accompany the film. In 1927, the first 'talkie' was released. 'Talkies' increased the demand for cinema even more.

Movie studios promoted their starring actors as well as their films. Actors were often presented as sex symbols to attract fans, and they were interviewed in magazines and made public appearances. Stars like Charlie Chaplin, Rudolf Valentino and Clara Bow quickly attracted fans who would pay to see their idol's films whatever the storyline, and whether or not the film was any good.

## The 'Jazz Age'

| What is jazz? | • Jazz is a musical style that combines several different musical types, including African spirituals, blues and brass band. |
|---|---|
| Where did it come from? | • It began among African-American musicians in the South. African Americans who moved to New York and Chicago to look for work brought jazz with them. |
| Why was jazz popular? | • Jazz was new and many people found the loud, lively music very exciting.<br>• Jazz music had a strong rhythm, which was good for dancing.<br>• Jazz rejected the rules of traditional music, and featured improvisation, which made every performance different. |
| What was different about jazz clubs? | • Jazz clubs attracted both black and white young people at a time when it was unusual for them to socialise together.<br>• Jazz music led to new dance styles. Formal dances like the waltz were replaced by the Charleston, the tango and the lindy-hop. |
| Did everyone like jazz? | • Jazz's African-American roots meant that some people thought it was immoral. Some even called it 'the Devil's music'. By the end of the 1920s, at least 60 communities had passed laws banning jazz in public dance halls. |

## Sport

Sport grew in popularity during the 1920s, and sports news was carried in newspapers, magazines and on the radio. Sportspeople like the baseball player Babe Ruth became celebrities and earned huge salaries from playing, and from endorsing products.

## An age of 'crazes'

The 'roaring twenties' was a time of rapidly changing crazes (something that is very popular for a short time).

There was a craze for playing the game mahjong, then for crosswords, book clubs, dance marathons – the list went on.

**Now try this**

You might also find page 2 helpful for this question.

Why do you think there was a growth in different kinds of entertainment in the 1920s? Explain your ideas in a short paragraph.

# Women in society

The 1920s were a period of great change – and this change affected American women, too. A particular change was women's position in society.

## The effects of the First World War

| Before the First World War | As a result of the First World War |
|---|---|
| • In the early 1900s, women had few opportunities. They couldn't vote and most couldn't work. | • When America joined the war in 1917, men left to fight and women took over the jobs that they left behind. |
| • Middle- and upper-class women had to obey many rules (for example, they were not allowed to be alone with men unless they were family members). | • Women got the vote in 1920. |
| • Make-up was forbidden and many women were discouraged from playing sports. | • Work gave women financial independence which meant that they had more options. |
| • Poorer women had to work, but they could only do low-paid, unskilled work. | • The divorce rate doubled in the 1920s as women realised that they did not have to stay in unhappy marriages. |

## Changes in dress and appearance

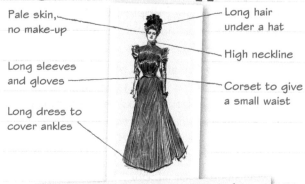

Pale skin, no make-up
Long hair under a hat
High neckline
Long sleeves and gloves
Corset to give a small waist
Long dress to cover ankles

Before the First World War, the ideal woman was the 'Gibson girl', made popular by the artist Charles Dana Gibson.

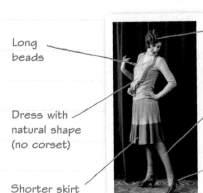

Long beads
Short hair, lipstick
Dress with natural shape (no corset)
Flesh-coloured stockings
Shorter skirt
High-heeled shoes.

A flapper in the 1920s.

## Flappers

• As women had more opportunities, the strict rules about 'proper' behaviour began to be relaxed.

• Many young women began to wear more revealing clothes, to smoke and drink (which were considered male habits), and to go out alone.

• They rode motorbikes and went dancing until the early hours of the morning. These young women became known as '**flappers**'.

Many older Americans were shocked by the flappers, and saw them as a symbol of the immorality of modern life. They thought the flappers were a direct attack on religious values and family life. There was even an 'Anti-Flirt League' to protest against the flappers and their 'immoral' behaviour!

Life was changing for some women in America, usually middle- and upper-class and living in the northern cities. Many other women found their lives changed very little – even though they could vote and work, they were not equal to men. Although around 10 million women had jobs in 1929, this was only 20% of women in America, and even then they were mainly in unskilled jobs and were paid less than men for the same work.

## Now try this

Give **two** examples of how women's position in society changed as a result of the First World War.

# Prohibition

In January 1920, the government passed a law that was immediately broken in practically every town in America. This law was known as 'prohibition' and it banned the sale, transport or manufacture of alcohol. The impact of prohibition on society was significant – it contributed to the sense of America as a divided society.

## Enforcing prohibition

1500 'Prohibition Agents' were employed to find out where alcohol was being made or sold. They then arrested the people responsible and confiscated the alcohol.

The agents also had to stop smugglers bringing alcohol into the country. This was not easy – the USA had about 18700 miles of border and coastline. Although the number of agents doubled between 1920 and 1930, they struggled to stop alcohol being smuggled from Canada and Mexico.

'Prohibition' was a nickname – officially it was the 18th amendment to the US Constitution.

It was not illegal to buy or drink alcohol – but it was illegal to make, transport or sell it.

## The case for prohibition

There had been campaigns against alcohol for several years before prohibition, led by groups such as the Anti-Saloon League, and supported by churches.

Opponents of alcohol claimed that it led to a decline in moral values and caused social problems like:

- violence and crime (including disorder and drink-driving)
- poverty and debt
- addiction and illness.

They thought a ban would make America a better country.

As a result of these campaigns, 33 states had already passed their own restrictions on alcohol. The new law made the ban complete and imposed it all over the country.

## The reaction to prohibition

- People liked to drink and wanted to buy alcohol – and there were people who were prepared to break the law to sell it to them. Many people felt that the government had no right to interfere in their private lives in this way.

- The demand for alcohol attracted criminals. Before long, gangs were running illegal bars called 'speakeasies' in basements and hotel rooms. During prohibition, New York had twice as many speakeasies as it had bars before 1920.

- Speakeasies got alcohol from 'bootleggers' who smuggled it into the country. This was called 'bootleg' alcohol. They also sold 'moonshine', a strong home-made spirit. Cases of alcohol poisoning increased by over 700%.

## Impact of prohibition: Gangsters and corruption

| Criminal gangs were soon making millions of dollars from smuggling and selling alcohol. |

⬇

| This meant that they could afford to bribe or intimidate police and judges to turn a blind eye. |

⬇

| Knowing they could buy off the law, the gangs began fixing races, running brothels and extorting money through protection rackets. |

⬇

| Because crime was so profitable, the gangs began to fight with each other. There were murders, gunfights and bombings. |

⬇

| Many people were frightened of the gangs and worried about official corruption. However, they didn't want to stop buying the alcohol that made the gangs so powerful. |

A protection racket involved offering to 'protect' businesses from damage in exchange for a fee – and if they didn't pay, smashing up their shops.

This became known as 'organised crime'. You can find out more on page 9.

## Now try this

Give **two** reasons why enforcing prohibition was difficult.

# Organised crime

Prohibition led to corruption and organised crime. In turn, organised crime had a significant impact on American society, creating more divisions. There were several crime organisations, but the Mafia was by far the biggest.

## Immigration and organised crime

During the nineteenth and early twentieth centuries, Italian immigrants came to America looking for a better life. There were 500000 Italians in New York City by 1910.

Most were farmers and unskilled labourers, although some were skilled craftsmen.

Most were law-abiding people, but any large group of people includes some criminals. Italian criminals tended to prey on the Italian community rather than other New Yorkers.

When Benito Mussolini became prime minister of Italy in 1922, he tried to get rid of the Italian **Mafia** (organised crime association).

Some Italian Mafia members escaped to the USA, where they became involved in bootlegging and ran gangs in American cities such as New York and Chicago. They became known as the American Mafia or 'the Mob'.

The St Valentine's Day Massacre: Al Capone wanted to get rid of his rival, George 'Bugsy' Moran, for control of bootlegging in Chicago. On 14 February 1929, Capone's gang killed seven members of Moran's gang. Moran escaped, but decided to retire.

## Impact on society

- **Gang violence**: Gangs fought each other for control of specific areas. These fights involved murder, gun battles and bombings, which frightened people nearby.

- **Intimidation**: The Mafia kept the Italian Mafia tradition of 'omerta' (silence and secrecy). The punishment for going to the police was death. Bars that refused to buy alcohol from the Mafia were blown up.

- **Spread**: The Mafia got everywhere. They fixed horse races, ran brothels and operated protection rackets. This made them even harder to challenge.

- **Corruption**: Mafia bosses like Al Capone bribed city mayors and the police, which protected them from law enforcement. This meant that many people felt that they could not trust the police or the authorities to protect them.

- **Suspicion of immigrants**: The Mafia made many people link immigration with crime.

### Al 'Scarface' Capone (1899–1947)

**Background:** Born in New York, the son of Italian immigrants. In 1919, Capone moved to Chicago and was offered a job by gang boss Johnny Torrio. He became Torrio's right-hand man and they took over other gangs, forming the 'Chicago Outfit'.

**Crime boss:** Torrio retired in 1925 and handed over to Capone. Capone expanded the business using more violent methods. He enjoyed his criminal reputation and showing off his wealth with clothes, jewellery and cigars. He gave money to charity and portrayed himself as a 'Robin Hood' figure. At one time he made $2 million a week.

**Trial and prison:** After the St Valentine's Day Massacre, public opinion swung against Capone. The FBI (US law enforcement) declared him 'Public Enemy No 1'. However, no witnesses to any of Capone's crimes could be persuaded to come forward. In the end, the police charged Capone with tax evasion, which needed no witnesses. Capone was sentenced to 11 years in prison.

## After prohibition

Prohibition had allowed organised crime to flourish, but the end of prohibition didn't mean the end of 'the Mob'. The criminal gangs simply moved into other areas, such as drug trafficking and illegal gambling. They also got involved in legitimate businesses such as construction and the clothing industry. The Italian Mafia is still operating today.

**Now try this**

Give **two** reasons why the FBI found it difficult to convict Al Capone for his 'Mob' activities.

# The experiences of immigrants

Between 1850 and the First World War, about 40 million people came to America hoping for a better life. Many were attracted by advertisements offering farmland, while others were escaping poverty or persecution. America was seen as a land of opportunity.

## Immigration from Europe

Immigration to America in the 19th and early 20th centuries was the biggest movement of people in history. The equivalent of 10% of the population of Europe came to America.

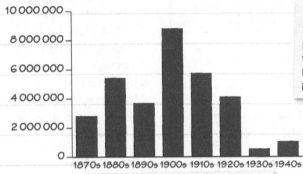

Number of immigrants by decade.

> In 1920, there were twice as many Irish people in New York as there were in Dublin! For more about the Irish immigrants, see page 1.

**2,000,000** FARMS of Fertile Prairie Lands to be had Free of Cost
**CENTRAL DAKOTA**
**30 Millions of Acres**
**YOU NEED A FARM!**
**CHICAGO and NORTHWESTERN**
**HOW TO GET THERE**
**Chicago & North-Western Ry.**

This poster from the 1870s encouraged migrants with the offer of free farmland in Dakota. As travel became easier, the government wanted people to settle in these areas and produce crops.

## Experiences of immigrants: expectation vs reality

| What immigrants expected | The reality of life in America |
|---|---|
| **Land**<br>• America is huge and there were millions of acres of cheap farmland.<br>• Immigrants were attracted by the offer of free 'homesteads' (land claimed under the Homestead Act of 1862). | **Land**<br>• Most of the land that was available was in the far West and South. These areas were remote and desolate – the journey there was dangerous and often took months.<br>• Life for homesteaders was extremely hard and many suffered extreme poverty. |
| **Work**<br>• America's new industries (such as cars and chemicals) and booming factories meant there were opportunities for work.<br>• Pay and conditions were generally better than in Europe. | **Work**<br>• Many immigrants found good jobs and others started successful businesses and made a good living.<br>• Some were not so lucky. Many were not well educated and spoke little English, and could find only low-paid jobs. |
| **The 'American Dream'**<br>America was founded on the principles of liberty and equality. The 'American Dream' was the idea that anyone who was prepared to work hard could be successful and wealthy. | **The 'American Dream'**<br>• Many immigrants worked hard but were still poor. They were often paid less than Americans.<br>• Many immigrants lived in poor housing due to poverty and prejudice. Thousands lived in slums in the early twentieth century.<br>• Despite the idea of equality in America, many immigrants faced prejudice from American citizens. |
| **Freedom**<br>The Declaration of Independence stated that all men had the right 'to life, liberty and the pursuit of happiness'. America had freedom of worship for people of all faiths. | **Freedom**<br>• This was attractive to many immigrants who did not have these freedoms at home, such as Eastern European Jews.<br>• This freedom did not protect immigrants from religious or political prejudice. |

### Now try this

Imagine you are an immigrant in America. Write a paragraph to describe your experience.
Give **one** reason why life isn't how you expected it would be.

# The impact of immigration

The first immigrants to America were generally welcomed. The impact of immigration began to change in the late nineteenth century, when 'new immigrant' groups began to arrive.

## The new immigrants

> The first immigrants were usually welcomed because they came from the same northern European countries as the original colonists. They were therefore not seen as 'foreign'.

> The immigrants who began to come to America in the late nineteenth century came from poorer countries of eastern and southern Europe. These immigrants were considered to be more 'foreign' and different.

> Many of these immigrants didn't plan to stay in America. Most of them were young men who hoped to stay for a few years and earn enough money to live a better life in their homeland.

> More than half of immigrants who came to America between 1880 and 1920 are believed to have eventually returned to their countries of origin. This lack of desire to become 'American' increased the feeling that the immigrants were different from Americans.

## Impact of immigration on society

By the 1920s, people in America spoke more languages and practised more religions than any other country in the world.

The 'new immigrants' rapidly formed new communities in major cities. Neighbourhoods called 'Little Italy', 'Greektown' and 'Irish Town' began to develop. These were close-knit communities with their own ethnic shops, banks, cinemas and restaurants. This gave immigrants a supportive network, but it often made integration into wider American society difficult.

The vast majority (at least 85%) of the American population was always people who had been born there. However, a concentration of immigrants in major cities created the feeling that foreigners were taking over. By 1920, more than 40% of the people in New York, Chicago and San Francisco had been born abroad.

## Causes of racial tension

The fact that many immigrants were seen as more 'foreign' contributed to prejudice against them. As a result, they were often blamed for social problems such as disease, crime, alcoholism and gambling.

- Because they were willing to work for low wages, immigrants were accused of 'stealing' work from Americans.
- Immigrants were used to break strikes and were blamed for worsening wages and working conditions.
- Immigrants also increased demand for scarce housing, so they were blamed for pushing up rents.
- The language barrier increased tension.
- Most old immigrants were Protestant and many new immigrants were Catholic or Jewish.

> Political differences caused tension too. Find out more on page 14.

## Government response to immigration

Suspicion of the new immigrant groups was shared by the government, who passed legislation to restrict the numbers allowed into America.

**1917:** Literacy rules meant that immigrants had to be able to read a 40-word sentence. This excluded uneducated migrants from Eastern Europe.

**1921:** Immigration Quota Law set a limit of 350000 immigrants a year. It also limited the numbers of immigrants from any country to 3% of the total population that was already in the USA. This was aimed at restricting the numbers from 'new immigrant' groups.

**1924:** The National Origins Act cut the number of immigrants to 150000 a year and reduced the national quota to 2%.

## Now try this

Give **two** examples of problems faced by new immigrants to America.

# Experiences of African Americans

All ethnic minority groups faced prejudice and discrimination, but it was particularly severe for African Americans. Slavery had been abolished in 1865, but in the 1920s, African Americans were still severely discriminated against by the white population.

## Racial division

After the abolition of slavery, the southern states where slaves had worked on cotton and tobacco plantations had a black majority. The white minority were frightened of the power that the black population would have if they were not 'controlled', so in 1877 they began to pass laws to keep African Americans **segregated** (separate) from white people. More and more of these laws were passed over the following decades. They were known as 'Jim Crow' laws, after an insulting name for an African American.

**The impact of racial division on African Americans**

African Americans could not use the same hotels, restaurants, swimming pools, water fountains or taxis as white people. They even had separate cemeteries.

Difficult 'literacy tests' were introduced to try to stop African Americans from voting.

Some states banned marriages between people of different races.

There were separate blood banks for black and white people.

Schools were segregated – black children had fewer teachers and resources.

Black people were only able to rent houses in less desirable neighbourhoods.

Black and white soldiers were segregated in the military.

## Lynching

Many black Americans were murdered (usually by hanging) for supposed 'crimes' without a trial. This was called '**lynching**'. Lynching had taken place since the end of slavery, but was still common in the 1920s – 61 people were lynched in 1921. The police mostly turned a blind eye. Most victims had done nothing wrong. Lynchings were often attended by thousands of people and sometimes postcards were sold showing the murder. The purpose of lynching was to show black Americans that white people were 'in control'. This idea is called '**white supremacy**' and was a key factor in creating racial division in American society.

Many lynchings were carried out by an organisation called the Ku Klux Klan. For more about the KKK, see page 13.

## Moving north

- Not surprisingly, many African Americans decided to leave the South.
- About 2 million of them – a sixth of the black population – moved north, where there were more jobs.
- They still faced discrimination, were paid less than white people, and had fewer opportunities, but things were still better than in the South.
- The black population of cities like New York and Chicago doubled between 1900 and 1920.

As black people moved north, they took their culture with them, especially their music. For more on this, see page 6.

## The NAACP

- ✓ In 1910, W.E.B. Du Bois, whose grandfather had been an African slave, set up the National Association for the Advancement of Colored People (NAACP).
- ✓ The NAACP campaigned for better rights for African Americans, such as better housing, the right to vote, and fairer laws.
- ✓ The political class of the 1920s did not accept any of the recommendations, but the NAACP became more influential in the 1960s. It still exists today.

For more about the NAACP and civil rights, see pages 29 and 30.

### Now try this

In no more than 40 words, explain how discrimination against African Americans contributed towards a divided society in the 1920s.

# The Ku Klux Klan

The 1920s was the time when a white supremacist group, the Ku Klux Klan, was at its strongest. The rise of the KKK is a clear example of the divisions in American society in the 1920s.

## What was the KKK?

The Ku Klux Klan was originally founded in the 1860s as a protest against the ending of slavery, usually through violence towards African-American leaders. It faded away within a few years, but regained strength in the early 1900s. In 1915, a film called *The Birth of a Nation* presented the KKK as protecting white people from violent black thugs. By 1921, the KKK had marketing staff and presented itself as a fraternal society (a group where members help each other). It was a secret, Protestant white-supremacist group which targeted African Americans, Jews, Catholics and immigrants. By 1925, there were about 5 million members, mainly in the southern states. Members wore white robes and hoods, used coded language and held secret ceremonies.

### The impact of the KKK

- ☑ The KKK's secrecy meant that black people were aware that any white person they met could be a member, which would have been very frightening.

- ☑ KKK members carried out activities aimed at intimidating black people, such as marches and cross-burnings, and took part in violence. Klan members were involved in many murders known as 'lynchings'. Other victims were beaten, whipped or attacked with acid or hot tar.

- ☑ Some police, judges and sheriffs were members, so actions were rarely punished. This increased the feeling that society was divided along race lines.

## Why did people join the KKK?

- Poor white people in the South and the West were angry that they were not seeing the rise in prosperity that had happened in the North. They looked for someone to blame.

- White people said that non-white people worked for lower wages, putting white workers out of a job.

- They saw themselves as defenders of the Protestant religion.

- They claimed to want to improve moral standards, and often attacked alcoholics, prostitutes and gamblers as well as immigrants.

- The KKK presented itself as a community organisation, giving opportunities for socialising.

- Some people were attracted by the secrecy and elaborate ceremonies.

- Some people were simply racist and saw the KKK as a way to express their racist beliefs.

## The decline of the KKK

- In 1925, David Stephenson, a Klan leader in Indiana, was convicted of kidnapping, raping and murdering a teacher called Madge Oberholtzer. He was sentenced to life imprisonment. During his trial, he revealed several KKK secrets. Membership began to decline rapidly.

- The KKK was damaged further in 1927, when a group of Klansmen in Alabama launched a wave of violent attacks on African Americans and also on white people they thought were immoral. Many people disapproved of these attacks and stopped supporting the KKK. By 1930, KKK membership had fallen from 5 million to 30000.

It is important to remember that the KKK still exists, and still promotes racism and white supremacy.

## Now try this

How did the influence of the KKK show that America in the 1920s was a divided society? Give a reason for your answer.

# The Red Scare

After the Russian Revolution in 1917, a fear and distrust of communism spread through America. This became known as the 'Red Scare'.

## Communist threat

- In 1917, a communist government was established in Russia. This was the beginning of the Soviet Union.
- Americans believed that there were many **anarchists** or communists in America. Many were frightened, especially as President McKinley had been assassinated by an anarchist in 1901.
- The fear of communism increased after a series of strikes in America in 1919. The communists usually got the blame for strikes, which the press presented as conspiracies against the government.
- The blame for strikes and the spread of revolutionary and anarchist ideas was pinned on southern and eastern European immigrants.

Compare this period with the Red Scare of the 1950s, on page 27.

**Anarchists** wanted to end traditional forms of government and allow people to form groups and decide how to run them. Although the communists and anarchists were different extreme groups, most Americans saw little difference between them.

## The Palmer raids

- In 1919, Alexander Mitchell Palmer became Attorney General (chief government lawyer).
- He claimed that communist agents were trying to overthrow the American government. The bomb attacks that Palmer had claimed were about to happen never came.
- On New Year's Day, 1920, Palmer ordered a series of raids on the homes of suspected communists and anarchists.
- Over 6000 people were arrested and put in prison. Many had to be released and only three guns were found in their homes.
- Apart from those arrested, very few people complained that these arrests weren't legal. They were so afraid of communism that they were prepared for the government to use illegal methods to tackle it.

After 1917, the Red Scare led to division in society because people were afraid of secret networks of communists and anarchists. This made them suspicious of other people, especially immigrants.

## The Sacco and Vanzetti case

Nicola Sacco and Bartolomeo Vanzetti were Italian immigrants. In May 1920 they were arrested and charged with a robbery in which two guards were killed.

⬇

As they didn't speak much English, they didn't understand much of what was said at their trial.

⬇

They were known to be anarchists and it is widely believed that this was why they were targeted.

⬇

The evidence against them was weak, but the judge at the trial said that whether or not they had committed the crime, they were still guilty because as anarchists they were enemies of the government!

⬇

Sacco and Vanzetti were found guilty and sentenced to death. They spent seven years in prison while their lawyers appealed. Despite many protests, both men were executed by electric chair in August 1927.

## The significance of the Sacco and Vanzetti case

- When the verdict was reported there was an outcry. There were strikes and protests because many people felt that the men's trial had been unfair.
- The protests continued long after the men had been executed. Protestors claimed that the case showed that the legal system was biased and that many people were not getting a fair trial.
- In December 1927 the state Judicial Council admitted that the trial had not been fair and proposed changes to the system to make sure it didn't happen again.

### Now try this

In no more than 140 characters, explain how the Sacco and Vanzetti case is evidence of a 'Red Scare'.

# The Wall Street Crash

In October 1929 the boom of the Roaring Twenties ended with a huge stock market crash. This was the beginning of what would become an economic **depression**.

A **depression** is when an economy collapses, causing high unemployment, difficulty in getting credit, people buying far less and far fewer goods being produced.

## What was the Wall Street Crash?

Throughout the 1920s, the American economy had been booming. Millions of people had bought shares, often with borrowed money.

During the boom there was huge demand for luxury goods such as cars, radios and fridges. But by 1929, nearly everyone who could afford them had bought them and more were being made than could be sold (overproduction).

Foreign governments had put high taxes on American products (often as payback for American import taxes) so the extra goods could not be sold elsewhere.

On 24 October 1929, 13 million shares were sold on the New York Stock Exchange – five times as many as usual. Share prices fell dramatically. This became known as 'Black Thursday'. Another 16 million shares were sold on 29 October.

As more companies began to look less profitable, more people sold their shares. The share price began to fall. This led to panic as people scrambled to sell shares before the price dropped further.

Company profits started to dip and a few people began to sell their shares because they were worried that they wouldn't get a dividend.

In the Wall Street Crash, American shares lost billions of dollars (89%) in value.

For more on the stock market, turn to page 5.

## Why did falling share prices cause a Depression?

- Many people had borrowed money to buy shares. When the share price collapsed, they couldn't repay their loans. The banks had also invested money in shares.

- The stock market crash caused banks to fail – more than 600 banks closed in 1929. The people who had put their life savings in the banks lost everything. Hundreds of thousands of people and businesses lost everything. This caused panic as people rushed to take their money out of the banks and caused more banks to fail.

- The banks that were left were very reluctant to lend money in case the people borrowing it couldn't repay their loans, so it became harder to borrow. Many businesses had to close, which meant many people lost their jobs.

- Unemployment meant that people had less money to spend, making it hard for them to buy food and pay rent.

### How does a bank work?

Banks have two functions – savings and loans:

**Savings** – People deposit money into a bank. In return, the bank pays them a small amount of interest.

**Loans** – The bank lends the savers' money to people who want to borrow it. They charge the borrower interest on the loan. This is how banks make a profit.

The Crash stopped banks working because when people removed their savings, the bank could no longer use the money to make loans. Other people could not repay their loans, so the banks ran out of money.

A branch of the Bank of the United States closed after the Crash. Huge numbers of people wanted their money back.

## Now try this

In a short paragraph, describe **at least two** effects of the Wall Street Crash on the American people.

# The Great Depression: impact

The Great Depression that followed the Wall Street Crash of 1929 hit American society hard and unemployment increased dramatically. Farmers and businessmen were among the groups affected.

## How did the Great Depression affect American society?

### Impact on business owners

- **Banks** had lent billions of dollars during the 1920s. Many borrowers couldn't pay it back, so banks went bankrupt.
- Banks were reluctant to lend money, making it harder for businesses to keep functioning.
- Between 1929 and 1932, industrial production fell by nearly 45%. Business profits dropped from $10 billion in 1929 to $1 billion in 1932.
- During the crash demand for goods fell away even more, meaning that businesses failed and factories closed.

The richest people in the country lost money in the Depression, but they were better off than most because they often had lots of property and land, which gave them an income. They did have to cut back on spending, and often did this by sacking staff.

### Unemployment

- Factories struggled and many eventually closed, leaving workers without jobs.
- Businesses supplying factories with raw materials such as steel, timber, textiles, rubber and leather also suffered, causing more factory closures and unemployment.
- Workers no longer used restaurants, shops and businesses near the factory, so these businesses began to struggle.
- In 1929, about 3% of Americans were unemployed. By 1932, 20000 companies had gone out of business and 13 million people – about 25% – of the workforce were unemployed.
- 34 million people were in families with no full-time wage earner. In some industrial cities, such as the car-making town of Toledo, Ohio, there was 80% unemployment.

To make matters worse, the closure of the banks meant that about 9 million people lost their life savings, so they had nothing to fall back on.

### Farmers

- During the boom farmers had borrowed money to buy new machinery. The new machinery meant they produced more food than they could sell, so food prices dropped.
- Struggling banks started demanding that farmers pay back their loans in full. Some could no longer afford to repay their debts and had to sack workers or sell their farms.
- Rising unemployment and poverty meant that demand for food fell further. Over 1 million families lost their farms between 1930 and 1934. Those who kept their land then had to struggle with drought. In the Midwest and southern plains, hot, dry weather combined with strong winds meant that millions of acres of topsoil were blown away, creating a Dust Bowl where crops could not grow. Many farmers abandoned their farms and moved away to try to find work. Most worked as labourers on other people's farms.

Many homeless people ended up in camps where they built houses from scrap materials. The camps became known as 'Hoovervilles', as people felt that President Hoover wasn't doing enough to help them. Charities set up kitchens where homeless people queued in 'breadlines' for soup and bread. By 1933, over 60% of Americans were categorised as poor by the government.

### Now try this

Which group do you think was most badly affected by the Depression? Explain your answer in a short paragraph.

# Hoover's response

Herbert Hoover became president in 1929 – a few months before October's Wall Street Crash. He thought the Depression was a short-term problem and in January 1930 he said America was over the worst. Hoover's response to the Depression made him very unpopular.

## Hoover's response to the Depression

Hoover's administration did try to solve the problems in the country's economy, but his belief in laissez-faire limited the amount of intervention he was prepared to make.

* He encouraged businesses to keep wages high to increase the amount available for buying goods. By 1931, however, businesses had no choice but to cut wages.

* Hoover introduced a two-cent tax on bank cheques to raise extra money for the government. People stopped using cheques and started using cash instead. Banks had already closed due to cash shortage, but this reaction to the tax rapidly increased the rate of bank closures.

* He introduced a $100 million fund to lend to farmers. However, this was a drop in the ocean, and many farmers were in too much debt to take on more loans.

* To combat unemployment among white Americans, he sent over 500 000 Mexicans and Mexican Americans to Mexico.

* He also supported new public works projects to create employment for construction workers.

* In June 1930, despite opposition from many economists, he introduced the Smoot–Hawley Tariff Act, which raised tax on many imported items. The idea was to encourage people to buy American products by increasing the cost of imported goods. However, economic depression had spread worldwide, and many nations responded by raising tariffs on American goods. This damaged international trade and made the Depression worse.

Hoover was US president from 1929 to 1933. He believed in the concept of 'rugged individualism', which meant that his response to the Depression did not help the people who needed it most.

For more on 'rugged individualism', turn to page 2.

## Hoover's unpopularity

* Hoover's belief in individualism meant that he vetoed (stopped) several bills that would have provided direct relief to struggling Americans. He argued that the government could not fix the problems by spending money.

* In 1930, the Republicans did badly in the elections to the House of Representatives (part of Congress). Despite the defeat, Hoover refused to change his policies.

* The American people became angry and unrest increased. Protests ranged from factory strikes to farm riots. In 1932, First World War veterans marched to Washington to receive their war pensions immediately, rather than waiting until 1945. Hoover refused and called in the military to disrupt the protest.

Many people thought that Hoover's refusal to provide direct relief was due to indifference or heartlessness, but this was not the case. He genuinely believed that 'rugged individualism' was the long-term solution to the Depression, and encouraged people to help each other rather than rely on the government. He thought that government intervention threatened individual freedom and wanted assistance to be handled on a voluntary basis. He practised what he preached – he didn't take a salary while president, and throughout the Great Depression, he donated an average of $25 000 every year to relief organisations.

## Now try this

In **no more than two** paragraphs, explain why Hoover had so little impact on the issues faced by the American people during the Depression.

# Roosevelt becomes president

In the 1932 presidential election, Herbert Hoover was challenged by a Democrat called Franklin Roosevelt. Roosevelt promised to do more to help America get out of the Depression.

### Franklin Delano Roosevelt (1882–1945)

Roosevelt (known as FDR) trained as a lawyer at Harvard University. During the First World War, he had a job in the Navy. In 1921 he caught polio (a disease of the spine) which nearly killed him. Although he recovered, he had to use a wheelchair for the rest of his life. In 1928, he went into politics as a member of the Democratic party and became Governor of New York.

## Laissez-faire vs New Deal

| Hoover's laissez-faire approach | Roosevelt's New Deal |
|---|---|
| • The electorate were familiar with Hoover's methods of dealing with the Depression. His 'hands-off' approach was very unpopular.<br><br>• After the Depression had run on for several years Hoover began to lend money to businesses and farms and make funding available for states to help the unemployed – but this was widely seen as too little, too late. | Roosevelt offered the American people what he called a 'New Deal' – a change from the laissez-faire approach taken by Hoover. The New Deal was focused on meeting the needs of the people affected by the Depression. It was made up of the 'three Rs':<br><br>• **Relief** – help for the unemployed, homeless, elderly and sick by providing money and temporary work<br><br>• **Recovery** – creating jobs by spending on large government schemes such as schools and roads<br><br>• **Reform** – permanent programmes to avoid another depression and protect people from economic disasters (such as protecting bank accounts). |

For more on Hoover's response to the Depression, see pages 16 and 17.

Hoover was very unpopular due to his laissez-faire approach to the Depression.

Some historians think that Roosevelt's reaching high office while managing a severe disability showed he had the personality to persevere through challenges.

Roosevelt was a very gifted public speaker whom audiences warmed to. Hoover disliked public speaking.

### Reasons for Roosevelt's victory

The New Deal offered by Roosevelt was popular with voters – many felt that Hoover was out of touch or uncaring.

Hoover had increased enforcement of prohibition. In contrast, Roosevelt promised to end prohibition – a promise that was very popular.

Roosevelt ran a very strong and effective campaign – he travelled all over the USA and made up to 15 speeches a day. His campaign theme tune was heard everywhere.

Roosevelt won the election by a landslide. There were 48 states in 1932, and he won 42 of them.

### Now try this

Did Roosevelt win the 1932 election or did Hoover lose it? Write a short paragraph explaining your answer.

# The start of the New Deal

Roosevelt had won the election by a landslide because he promised a 'New Deal' for the American people. His policies aimed to support many different groups in American society. When he took office, he promised 'action, and action now'.

## Roosevelt's first 100 days

Roosevelt kept his promise. When he took office in March 1933, he took three main actions.

| Restoring trust in the banks | Finding money to help the unemployed | Ending prohibition |
|---|---|---|
| **The problem:** Over 5000 banks closed during the Depression, and millions of people lost their savings. This meant that people no longer trusted banks. They panicked and kept their money at home – so banks could not lend to people wanting to start businesses. | **The problem:** Roosevelt needed to take immediate action to help the unemployed but there was no money. | **The problem:** Prohibition was unpopular, had led to organised crime and police corruption, as well as social problems. |
| **The solution:** Emergency Banking Act 1933. The Act closed all banks for four days so they could be inspected to make sure they were well-run, honest and solvent (had enough money to operate). Only those that passed the test could re-open. | **The solution:** Economy Act 1933. This cut pay for people working for the government and armed forces by 15%. | **The solution:** Beer Act 1933. This made it legal to make and sell alcohol again. |
| **Did it work?** Yes. $1 billion was paid into bank accounts when the banks opened. | **Did it work?** Yes. This made nearly $1 billion available for the New Deal. | **Did it work?** Yes. Although it didn't end organised crime, it did reduce the power of the gangs. It also created jobs and made money for the government through taxing alcohol. |

## The 'Alphabet Agencies'

Roosevelt knew that getting America out of the Depression would be hard – and that he didn't know exactly what to do. He recruited lots of expert advisers (he called them the 'Brain Trust') and started over 100 new organisations to tackle different problems.

These new organisations were known by their initials. They were nicknamed the 'Alphabet Agencies' because there were so many of them. These are just some of the key examples.

**Some of the 'Alphabet Agencies'**

**Farmers:** AAA – Agricultural Adjustment Agency – paid farmers to produce less, which led to raised prices and better incomes for farmers.

**Industry:** NRA – National Recovery Administration – encouraged workers and employers to agree fair wages and conditions, and gave workers the right to join trade unions.

**Unemployed:** FERA – Federal Emergency Relief Agency – gave $500m to states to provide help to the homeless and malnourished by funding soup kitchens, blankets and clothes. It also provided childcare so parents could find work.

## 'Priming the pump'

Roosevelt's theory was that by spending money he could kick-start the economy. In other words, if the government created work, people would spend their wages and businesses would expand, creating more jobs and more prosperity. This idea is sometimes called 'priming the pump'.

## 'Fireside chats'

Roosevelt made great use of the radio as a form of communication. He made 28 radio broadcasts explaining his policies. The first was about the banking crisis, and was made eight days into his presidency. The broadcasts were in the evening, and they were clear and conversational. Roosevelt called them his 'fireside chats' and they made him very popular.

## Now try this

Which **one** of the three main actions Roosevelt took in his first 100 days was most significant? Explain your answer in a short paragraph.

# Opposition to the New Deal

Not everyone was in favour of Roosevelt's New Deal. Some people, like Hoover, believed that people should look after themselves, while others thought that more should be done.

## The rich

- Roosevelt funded the New Deal by increasing taxes on the wealthy, and many of them did not like it. They thought the government was wasting money by paying people to plant trees and paint buildings.

- They also felt that they had lost enough – many had lost a lot of money in the Wall Street Crash. Roosevelt understood this, but said that they had something left, so should help those who had nothing.

- Many business owners resented the way that Roosevelt's policies interfered in business – for example, increasing workers' rights by setting minimum wages and maximum hours of work.

A cartoon from 1935 opposing the New Deal. It shows a 'tax burden' – the costs of Roosevelt's policies – sinking a boat called 'Business', with the 'Taxpayer' struggling at the helm.

## Political opposition: Republicans

Many Republicans, like Hoover, believed that people should solve their own problems. They thought that the New Deal policies were having too much influence on people's lives and that the government was getting too powerful. Some accused Roosevelt of being a dictator, while others thought that America was heading towards communism.

## Political opposition: radical politicians

Some politicians took the opposite view – that the New Deal didn't go far enough and that the government should be doing **more**. Francis Townsend suggested a retirement age of 60 to make jobs for young people. Charles Coughlin's National Union for Social Justice said that Roosevelt should do more to create jobs and ensure higher wages for workers.

One radical politician, Huey Long, said that there should be a 'Share Our Wealth' policy: any fortunes over $5 million should be confiscated and shared out, every family would have a car, a house and a radio, and there would be free education and cheap food for the poor. His ideas were very popular!

## Opposition from the Supreme Court

The Supreme Court is America's highest court. It decides whether new laws obey the Constitution. According to the Constitution, the President can make laws affecting the whole country, and individual state governments decide on laws for their own states.

In 1935, the Supreme Court decided that the Agricultural Adjustment Agency was unconstitutional (did not follow the Constitution) because it took away the states' rights to decide what money to give farmers. It also said that some of the measures introduced by the National Recovery Administration were illegal for the same reason.

For more on the Constitution, see page 1.

For more on the AAA, see page 19.

### The 1936 election

Despite opposition to the New Deal, Roosevelt won the 1936 election easily – even though the Republicans chose a very popular politician to run against him. This was because, although the people who opposed Roosevelt's policies were very vocal, the majority of American people benefited from the New Deal.

## Now try this

Roosevelt said that everyone was against the New Deal except the voters. In a short paragraph, explain what he meant by this.

# Evaluating Roosevelt's New Deal

To evaluate Roosevelt's contribution as president, it is necessary to look at the successes of the New Deal and its limitations.

## What economic changes did the New Deal bring?

| | Success | Limitation |
|---|---|---|
| Jobs | The New Deal created jobs – unemployment fell from 14 million in 1933 to under 8 million by 1937. | It didn't solve the problem of unemployment completely. Unemployment was still about 10%. There wasn't full employment until the Second World War. |
| Wealth | America's GNP (Gross National Product, the sum of all wealth created in a country) rose from $442 per capita (per person) in 1932 to $701 in 1937. | Although the economy as a whole improved, the benefits were not shared equally. Some people's lives improved far more than others' and poverty was still a social problem. |
| Farmers | Roosevelt tried hard to support farmers by raising crop prices and lending them money to protect them from losing their farms. | Most of this help went to larger farms, and small-scale farmers did not benefit as much. The Supreme Court's judgement that the AAA was unconstitutional meant that it was unable to help as much as intended. |
| Banks | The number of bank failures fell dramatically – more than 4000 in 1933 to fewer than 100 in 1934. | Turn to page 16 for a reminder of the problems America was facing as a result of the Great Depression. |

## What social changes did the New Deal bring?

| | Success | Limitation |
|---|---|---|
| Unemployment and poverty | The New Deal did make many Americans better off. In 1935 the Social Security Act made sure that anyone who was out of work got government help. This provided security while jobs were still being created. | However, tackling poverty was still a priority for Kennedy and Johnson in the 1960s. <br><br> Changes in unemployment and poverty are also linked to economic change. |
| Workers | Workers' rights were protected with a minimum wage, which gave security to people who were worried about being able to support themselves and their families, and by the Wagner Act (1935), which gave workers the right to join a union. | There were no New Deal programmes aimed at women – and the NRA rules set lower wages for women than for men. |
| Native Americans | The Indian Reservation Act of 1934 meant that Native Americans could run their reservations themselves, for example, running their own law courts. | However, this did not stop many Native Americans suffering poverty and discrimination. |

## A popular President

Franklin D. Roosevelt was one of the most popular presidents in American history. He was elected four times (1932, 1936, 1940 and 1944). His New Deal is still considered to be one of most important examples of direct government involvement in the economy America has ever seen.

To answer this question, you need to think about:
- How far Roosevelt achieved his aims (the 3 Rs of Relief, Recovery and Reform).
- If he didn't achieve all he intended, was there still enough improvement to describe it as a success?

### Now try this

Do you think the New Deal was a success or not? Give **two** reasons for your answer.

# Popular culture in the 1930s

The Roaring Twenties had been a time of rapid changes in popular culture. The Depression of the 1930s affected popular culture in America too, with developments in areas such as music, cinema, literature and sport.

For more on the popular culture of this time, see page 6.

## What is 'popular culture'?

**Popular culture** reflects what most people are interested in. It is influenced and spread by mass media. People experience it by hearing popular music, watching television or going to the cinema, playing or watching sports and reading popular books and magazines, following fashion and using new technology.

Historians study popular culture because it gives an insight into the way people thought and acted at the time, and their attitudes to religion, politics and society.

## Government and the arts

Roosevelt wanted artists of all types to continue to work throughout the Depression. He set up the Works Progress Administration (WPA) which employed artists in many ways:

- **writers** produced books on the history and traditions of each state
- **artists** painted murals in public buildings
- **actors** put on free theatre performances.

Some people felt the WPA was a waste of money, but the programmes made many Americans more knowledgeable about their history and culture.

## What was popular culture like in the 1930s?

### Music

Jazz performers such as Billie Holiday and Duke Ellington were still very popular. People still went to concerts and clubs, but more people listened to music on the radio, too, and buying records became popular.

### Cinema

Cinema was as popular during the Depression as it had been in the 1920s – about 60 million people went to the movies every week. People wanted to forget the troubles of the Depression, so films that offered an escape from real life were popular, such as:

- musicals (*42nd Street, Showboat, The Wizard of Oz*)
- comedies (the films of Charlie Chaplin, and Laurel and Hardy)
- historical dramas (*Gone with the Wind, Robin Hood*)
- horror (*King Kong, Dracula*).

### Comics

The first comic books or 'comics' were published in 1933, but they became wildly popular in 1938 when Action Comics appeared, featuring the introduction of Superman.

Comics were popular because they were cheap, cheerful and offered an easy method of escape for young people tired of the Depression.

### Literature

The 1930s were a golden age for American literature. Some of the country's most famous books were produced during – and inspired by – the Depression. For example:

- John Steinbeck's *The Grapes of Wrath* (1939) tells the story of an Oklahoma family whose farm is destroyed by a severe drought. *Of Mice and Men* (1937) describes two ranch workers who move around California in search of work.
- Erskine Caldwell's *Tobacco Road* (1932) describes the poverty of a Southern tenant farming family whose lives become desperate as the Depression worsens.
- Henry Roth's *Call It Sleep* (1934) follows an immigrant boy growing up in the New York slums.
- *They Shoot Horses, Don't They?* (1935) by Horace McCoy is set during a dance marathon during the Great Depression.

### Sports

During the Depression, attendance at football and baseball games fell sharply. As ticket income fell, promoters and athletes looked for other ways to make money, and sponsorship became a common form of advertising. However, more people began to play sport, as unemployed people had more free time.

The increasing popularity of radio meant that more people followed sports events via radio broadcast.

## Now try this

Give **three** examples of how the Great Depression affected American popular culture.

# Economic recovery

The USA started fighting in the Second World War in 1941, two years after it began. However, from its beginning in 1939, the war had a huge impact on the country's economy.

## How did the war help the economy to recover?

### Challenges to isolationism

After the First World War, the USA followed a policy called **isolationism** (not getting involved in other countries' affairs). It had focused on building its own economy and trading network. In 1935, with tension in Europe rising, the **Neutrality Act** banned loans to countries at war, and in 1937, arms sales to warring countries were banned.

In 1937, Roosevelt argued that aggressive nations should be challenged by countries who wanted peace. It was obvious that he was talking about Germany, Italy and Japan.

When the Second World War broke out in 1939, America declared support for Britain and France. This was because:

- They feared that if Germany defeated Britain and France, the USA could be attacked next.
- Japanese hostility threatened American markets in the Far East, which the government wanted to protect.

After the neutrality laws were changed, Roosevelt persuaded Congress to help the **Allies** (Britain and France) against Germany by exporting supplies to them. This not only helped the Allies, it also boosted the American economy.

### Exports: Cash and Carry Plan

- In 1939, Britain and France bought American weapons and aeroplanes under the 'Cash and Carry Plan'. America could sell these goods as long as the nation buying them paid immediately in cash, and transported the goods themselves, taking on the risk of transport.
- These exports boosted the American economy by creating manufacturing jobs and providing valuable income, while allowing America to stay neutral.
- In 1940, however, Germany invaded France and seemed on the point of defeating Britain, which was very short of money. FDR abandoned neutrality and gave Britain 50 ships.

FDR was elected President for a third time in 1940. By 1941, unemployment was half the 1937 level, partly due to production of goods for the Second World War.

### Lend Lease

- In March 1941, Roosevelt agreed a 'Lend Lease' arrangement with Britain. Instead of selling weapons, America would lend them $7000 million worth of arms. The weapons could be used until they were returned or destroyed but most people knew that America would get very little of the equipment back.
- In return, the Allies repaid the loan with gold, and by allowing American aircraft to use their air bases. The deal also created a huge number of manufacturing jobs.
- Not everyone supported Lend-Lease. Some people and organisations feared that it meant that America was at risk of being dragged into the war. Eventually, America began to rearm in case it had to join in – and millions of people were employed making planes, tanks and ships, and thousands more joined the armed forces.

### America enters the war

On the morning of 7 December 1941, Japanese bombers attacked Pearl Harbor: 21 warships and 177 planes were lost, and over 2000 men were killed. On 8 December, America declared war. America's isolationism was over. This provided a further boost to the economy. Military production increased and unemployment fell further as men joined the armed forces.

- In January 1942, the month after America entered the war, the government set up the War Production Board (WPB) to convert peacetime industries to war production.
- Car companies made tanks and planes and garment factories made parachutes.
- The WPB made sure factories had what they needed. FDR set a target of 50 000 aeroplanes a year. In 1944 American factories produced 96 000 – nearly double the target.
- In 1939, unemployment was at 17% – 9.5 million Americans had no job. By 1941, half of them were in jobs making planes, ships and tanks. By 1944, unemployment was below 2%.
- Farmers, who had struggled during the Depression, were now providing food for the army.

## Now try this

Describe **three** ways in which the Second World War helped the American economy to recover.

# Social developments

The Second World War had an enormous impact on the American economy, but it also caused massive social changes, especially for women and African Americans.

## Women

- Only 1 in 5 American women had a job in 1929, and although some women did manage to pursue careers in the law or medicine, most of those who did work outside the home either did unskilled work or 'feminine' jobs like teaching or nursing. Many women found that they were expected to give up their jobs when they got married.

- In 1941, with men going away to fight, women had more opportunities to work. They began to take jobs in factories, shipyards and on the railways, and made up a third of America's workforce. This gave them financial independence and more freedom. Involvement in the workplace meant that many women felt that they were more involved in society and political engagement among women increased.

She's a **WOW** WOMAN ORDNANCE WORKER

350 000 women joined the armed forces. More than 75 000 women served as army or navy nurses. 150 000 women joined the WAAC (Women's Auxiliary Army Corps). 84 000 WAVES (Women Accepted for Volunteer Emergency Service) joined the Naval Reserve.

American WW2 poster encouraging women to work in weapons factories. The red and white spotted headscarf of the 'Woman Ordnance Worker' (WOW) is shown alongside the caps worn by female members of the armed forces. The message is that the WOW is as important to the war effort as the women who joined the military.

## The impact of the Second World War on African Americans

| African Americans in the military | The war and civil rights |
|---|---|
| • About a million African Americans served in the armed forces during the Second World War. Despite this, they faced discrimination. | • In 1941, civil rights campaigner A. Philip Randolph organised a huge march on Washington. It was a protest against the defence industries' exclusion of African Americans and other minorities, and against segregation in the military. |
| • Before the Second World War, black soldiers could not become officers because some people believed that white soldiers could not be expected to obey a black officer. Black sailors were only allowed to work in ships' kitchens. The air force would not allow black pilots. African-American women could become army nurses, but they could only treat black soldiers. | • Roosevelt wanted to avoid thousands of angry protestors descending on Washington, so he said that any firm that had a contract with the government could not discriminate. He established the Fair Employment Practice Committee (FEPC) to investigate discrimination. The FEPC couldn't force companies to employ African Americans, but could recommend they didn't get government contracts if they didn't. |
| • As the war progressed, discrimination against black servicemen began to ease. In 1941, the first black pilots were trained but they had to fight in separate squadrons. Black soldiers were allowed to become officers for the first time, but were segregated into black-only units and could not command white troops. | • After the war, the role African Americans had played in the war was recognised by President Harry S. Truman who ordered racial equality in the military (1948). The work of the FEPC contributed to the fight for civil rights. |

The Congress of Racial Equality (CORE) was formed during the war and was important in the fight for civil rights in the 1950s and 1960s. You can revise the civil rights movement on pages 29–32.

## Now try this

Give **one** example of how the Second World War led to social developments in America.

# Consumerism and prosperity

After the end of the Second World War in 1945, America entered a period of social change and economic prosperity, guided by President Roosevelt's successor, Harry S. Truman.

**Consumerism:** The efficient manufacturing systems set up during the war were now used to produce consumer goods like cars, TVs and domestic appliances cheaply. Demand was high as these goods had been unaffordable during the Depression and the war.

**'GI Bill':** This 1944 law provided help to war veterans (a 'GI' was an American soldier). They were offered cheap loans to buy houses, and grants to attend college or learn a trade. Veterans were given $4 billion by the federal government between 1944 and 1949.

**Korean War:** Between 1950 and 1953 America was involved in a war in South East Asia. America supported South Korea, while the USSR (Soviet Union) supported North Korea. The conflict increased tension between the USA and USSR, in what was known as the Cold War. Because of this, America continued military spending: producing weapons, and boosting the steel, electronic and chemical industries.

**Causes of prosperity**

**Truman's 'Fair Deal':** Truman shared Roosevelt's belief that the government should help people in need and try to make society fairer. Truman introduced a 'Fair Deal' between 1945 and 1953, aimed at tackling poverty and inequality. Slum housing was replaced and the minimum wage was raised from 40 cents to 75 cents an hour, putting more money in the pockets of the poorest workers.

**Eisenhower's business-focused government:** In 1952, America elected a new president – the Republican Dwight 'Ike' Eisenhower – who brought businessmen into government to help boost the economy.

**Exports:** As Europe recovered from the Second World War, demand for American goods increased, making exports a huge source of wealth.

## The effects of consumerism

- Consumerism created a huge advertising industry, including on TV, which in turn created demand for consumer goods.
- Companies offered 'buy now, pay later' schemes.
- Huge malls (shopping centres) were built on the edges of towns and cities. Out-of-town shopping caused town centres to decline.
- By the mid-1950s, there were 75 million vehicles in America. Many more roads and car parks were built.
- Widespread car ownership and better roads led to large housing developments in the suburbs.
- Thanks to low housing costs, wage rises, and cheap loans offered under the GI Bill, many Americans could afford to buy their own homes.
- Manufacturing methods perfected during the war were now used in house building. Thousands of almost identical houses were built using mass production.

## The post-war 'baby boom'

- The birth rate in the USA rose dramatically after the Second World War: between 1944 and 1961, more than 65 million children were born.
- Many couples had waited to get married until the end of the war, or had not been able to afford to have a family during the Depression. Peacetime, and increased prosperity, made people more keen to have children.
- The GI Bill meant that many veterans could afford to settle down, buy houses and learn a trade, which also contributed to the baby boom. The people born during this period became known as 'baby boomers'.

### Now try this

Give **three** examples of ways that government policy contributed to increased prosperity in the post-war period.

# The American Dream

The 'American Dream' is the idea that in America anyone can succeed as long as they work hard enough. This idea had been attracting immigrants to the country since the nineteenth century. In the 1950s, America was the richest country in the world, and more people were living the **American Dream** than ever before. However, not everyone benefited.

## Did everyone experience the American Dream?

- Despite the rising prosperity in post-war America, there were still significant inequalities.

- President Truman had tried to tackle some of the inequalities with his 'Fair Deal'. He had some success replacing slum housing and raising the minimum wage, but some of his other policies were not introduced.

- Access to healthcare was patchy and not everyone could afford medical treatment. Truman, a Democrat, wanted to introduce health provision, but this was blocked by Republicans.

- The African-American population suffered low pay, poor housing and widespread discrimination, but southern politicians voted against Truman's attempts to improve the lives of black Americans.

## Poverty

Although the economy was booming, about a quarter of Americans were living in poverty in the 1950s.

- African Americans were hit harder by poverty than other groups – more than half of them lived in poverty, compared to 18% of white Americans.

- The north and west coasts were much better off than the South, where most African Americans lived.

- Older people were also suffering – in 1960, more than two thirds of people over 65 were living on less than a quarter of the average factory wage.

- Most Native Americans also lived in poverty, had less access to education, and were forced to live on reservations with poor-quality land.

**Changing roles:** Many women had done valuable work during the war, but once the war ended they were expected to go back to their traditional role as housewives and mothers.

**Marriage:** By 1950, the average age for women getting married had dropped to 20, the lowest since the nineteenth century.

**Falling wages:** Women who kept their jobs saw their wages fall from 66% of the male wage to 53%.

## Women's lives

**Motherhood:** The 'baby boom' meant that many women were having more children. At the time childcare fell to mothers so larger families increased this burden.

See page 24 for more on women's work during the Second World War, page 25 for the 'baby boom' and page 35 on the feminist movement and the demand for women's rights.

**Jobs:** Many women who wanted to pursue a career were confined to traditionally 'feminine' roles like nursing or secretarial work – women who tried to become managers faced extreme discrimination. By the late 1950s, many women were becoming frustrated and dissatisfied with the lack of opportunities open to them.

You might find it helpful to refer to pages 24 and 25 when answering this question.

### Now try this

'In the 1950s, the American Dream wasn't real, it was a myth – it didn't actually exist.' Decide whether you agree with this statement, and give **two** reasons for your answer.

# McCarthyism

In the 1950s a **Red Scare** (fear about the spread of communism) swept through America. Investigations by senator Joseph McCarthy led to the period becoming known as McCarthyism.

This fear had happened before. See page 14 for more about the Red Scare of the 1920s.

**The Cold War (1947–91):** The USSR, which was communist, became a rival to America as a **superpower** (a very powerful, influential country). Tensions grew worse after the USSR began testing nuclear weapons in 1949.

**Korean War (1950–53):** American help during the war in Korea was intended to challenge communist advances in South East Asia – but the war was going badly.

**Causes of the 'Red Scare' in the 1950s**

**Spy scandals:** In 1950, a government employee called Alger Hiss was accused of spying for the USSR. In 1953, two Americans (Julius and Ethel Rosenberg) were executed for spying. The public became frightened about the possibility of communism spreading to America.

**Communism spreads:** America adopted a policy called **containment**, which aimed to stop the spread of communism. Communist advances in Eastern Europe and China made it look like containment wasn't working.

## 'Un-American Activities'

The 'House Un-American Activities Committee' (HUAC) was set up in 1938 to investigate claims of disloyalty and trouble-making against people and organisations with suspected links to communism.

In 1945, the HUAC became a permanent committee and its role was expanded to allow it to investigate influential people suspected of being communists.

Between 1947 and 1950, millions of Americans were investigated for communist sympathies. None of them were ever convicted of spying, but even being investigated cost most of them their jobs.

## McCarthyism and its effects

### Joseph McCarthy and McCarthyism

In 1950, senator Joseph McCarthy claimed that he had the names of over 200 communist spies employed by the government. This caused a sensation and, in a country terrified of communism, McCarthy became a hero.

Between 1950 and 1955, McCarthy led an increasingly frantic series of investigations to root out supposed communists. He rarely had any real evidence for his claims. Anyone who opposed him was accused of being a communist supporter. McCarthy made it clear that the only way you could prove you had abandoned 'left-wing views' (even if you had never been communist) was by naming other members of the party.

His researchers investigated libraries and discovered 30 000 books that they thought were 'communist'. These books were removed from library shelves.

### Effects on American society

- Left-wing groups began to disappear as their ideas became associated with communism. Many left-wing people left America. This caused an imbalance in American politics.

- Politicians were afraid to oppose McCarthy because their careers would be harmed if they were suspected of being communist. Even President Eisenhower was afraid of working with McCarthy's enemies.

- Some filmmakers and writers who did not want to answer questions about their political beliefs were jailed, and didn't work in Hollywood again. This meant that others became reluctant to deal with controversial social or political issues.

- In the name of protecting America from communists, the government attacked individual rights and started to control organisations that had been independent.

### McCarthy's downfall

Eventually, McCarthy's investigations went too far. He accused 45 army officers of being communists. He was asked to provide proof and failed to do so. At the same time, army officials fed anti-McCarthy stories to the press. Public support for McCarthy fell quickly and many people disapproved of his methods. People started to use the term 'McCarthyism' to describe the act of making accusations without evidence, and the term is still used today.

## Now try this

Why do you think there was such a fear of communism in America in the 1950s? Give **three** reasons.

# The Rock and Roll generation

Children born in the 'baby boom' had a very different upbringing to their parents. This led to changes in popular culture, such as the arrival of television and rock and roll.

For more on popular culture, see page 22.

## New possibilities

- During the Depression and the Second World War, many families struggled financially, and many 14- and 15-year-olds left school to help support the family.
- After the war was over, parents who had lived through it wanted better opportunities for their children.
- Increased prosperity meant that children did not need to work, and many stayed in school longer or went on to university.

## Features of popular culture

- Young people are often the first to consume popular culture, for example in music, television and cinema.
- New trends start in one area, and spread rapidly to large numbers of people.
- It is constantly changing and evolving, mixing in new ideas.
- It includes commercial products (such as merchandising) and the growing demand for those products.

## How did popular culture change?

### Teenagers

- The word 'teenagers' was introduced in the 1950s to describe the new group of young people who had more spare cash – and more free time to spend it – than previous generations. This reflected the increased prosperity in society as well as changes in social attitudes.
- Teenagers spent their money on clothes, records, eating out, entertainment and, increasingly, alcohol. American businesses soon realised that teenagers had money to spend, so they started targeting more products and advertising at young people.

In 1940, the average 15-year-old had $1–2 a week to spend. By the late 1950s, this had risen to around $15.

### A 'generation gap'

- The popular culture aimed at and consumed by teenagers meant that they soon dressed, spoke and behaved differently to their parents. They listened to different music and enjoyed doing different things. Parents often struggled to understand their children and a **generation gap** (difference in attitudes between the generations) developed.
- Many older Americans thought that teenagers were rude, rebellious and disrespectful. Film stars like James Dean became symbols of teenage rebellion.

James Dean on the set of *Rebel Without A Cause* (1955). The promotional poster described it as a film about 'today's teenage violence'.

### Rock and Roll

- Rock and Roll was a new style of music that became popular in the 1950s. It developed from blues and jazz, but was made for a largely white audience, who had more money to spend.
- Its strong rhythm made it easy to dance to, and the lyrics often referred to young people doing things like staying out late and drinking. Many older Americans thought rock and roll was immoral and dangerous – which of course made teenagers like it even more!

### Television

- In 1950, about 3 million families had a television. Ten years later, this had risen to 55 million. The price of a television set dropped from $500 to $200.
- Television presented an 'ideal' family life from an almost entirely white point of view. It showed adverts that encouraged people to buy products to be like the people they saw on TV, and influenced every aspect of culture.

## Now try this

Give **three** examples of how popular culture changed during the 1950s.

# Segregation and civil rights

Despite rising prosperity and huge social change, in the 1950s African Americans were still living under the same Jim Crow laws that had segregated them in the 1920s.

## The civil rights movements

The civil rights movement is the name given to a campaign for equality between white Americans and African Americans. It began in the 1940s with the founding of the Congress of Racial Equality (CORE). CORE played an important role in the civil rights movement and led to the Civil Rights Act of 1968.

> The Jim Crow laws demanded 'separate but equal' segregation between black and white people in public places, schools and transportation, as well as for restaurants, bathrooms and drinking fountains. In practice, they weren't equal at all. For more on Jim Crow laws and segregation, see page 12.

Demands from African Americans involved in the civil rights movement included:

- an end to segregation
- equal access to housing and education
- an end to discrimination in employment
- an end to restrictions on voting.

## Brown vs Topeka

### Timeline

**Feb 1951** Case of Brown vs Board of Education of Topeka is filed in Kansas.

**Aug 1951** Judge **upholds** (supports) the Education Board's segregation policy.

**Nov 1951** The NAACP appeals the decision in the Supreme Court.

**Dec 1952** The Supreme Court hears arguments that segregated schools violate the Constitution.

**June 1952** The Supreme Court orders all cases to be reargued in 1953.

**Dec 1953** After a second round of arguments, the Supreme Court discusses school desegregation.

**May 1954** The Court finds school segregation to be unjust.

**May 1955** The Supreme Court declares that desegregation should proceed quickly.

**1961** After her father's death, Linda Brown becomes a civil rights advocate.

> Brown vs Topeka was brought by several African-American parents, after Oliver Brown's daughter Linda was not allowed to enrol in the (white) school nearest her home.

## The murder of Emmett Till

Emmett Till was a 14-year-old African American. In 1955, a white woman called Carolyn Bryant claimed that he had flirted with her (she later admitted he hadn't). Bryant's husband and brother-in-law brutally murdered Till. The murder was a graphic example of the impact of segregation.

Emmett's mother insisted on having an open coffin so that everyone would see her son's mutilated body. However, Emmett's killers were acquitted. The case drew attention to the violent persecution of African Americans. Till became an icon of the civil rights movement.

## Little Rock High School, 1957

In 1955, following Brown vs Topeka, the Supreme Court ordered that all schools should be **desegregated** (stop segregation). However, there was resistance in several southern states, where White Citizens' Councils were set up to stop it. In September 1957, the NAACP registered nine black students (later called the Little Rock Nine) to attend Little Rock High School.

However, the governor of Arkansas, Orville Faubus, opposed desegregation and sent state troops to stop the students from entering the school at the start of term. A huge angry crowd were protesting as well. The students only got into the school because President Eisenhower intervened. The legal battle continued for over a year before the students were able to go to school in 1959. Even when they did so, they faced hostility and abuse.

### Now try this

Give **four** ways in which the lives of African Americans were affected by segregation and discrimination in the 1950s.

# Peaceful protest 1

The 1954 Supreme Court ruling in Brown vs Topeka was a major boost for the civil rights movement, and began a wave of peaceful protest.

## The Montgomery Bus Boycott

Although the Supreme Court ruled in 1954 that black and white children should be educated together, many other services were still segregated. African Americans continued to suffer violent oppression.

On 1 December 1955, an African-American woman called Rosa Parks refused to give up her seat on a bus to a white man. Driven in part by the murder of Emmett Till in July 1955 (see page 29), she was arrested and fined for breaking city laws.

On 5 December, Martin Luther King Jr led a boycott of Montgomery buses that went on for several months. Since African Americans made up three quarters of bus passengers, this caused the bus company to suffer financial difficulties.

The protestors received threats, and in 1956 King's house was bombed. Some of the activists wanted to fight back, but King told them that peaceful direct action was the only way that they could win the fight for civil rights.

Rosa Parks was not the first person to refuse to give up her seat, but her refusal to accept segregation encouraged other civil rights activists to campaign against it. She was the secretary of the Montgomery NAACP and understood the principles of non-violent protest. As she was a married, respectable woman, it was difficult for people to criticise her behaviour.

## Martin Luther King Jr (1929–68)

Martin Luther King giving a speech in Selma, Alabama in 1965.

King became a Baptist minister in 1954 at the age of 25. His faith influenced his belief in non-violent protests such as sit-ins and boycotts. He called this 'direct action'.

In 1957 King co-founded the Southern Christian Leadership Conference (SCLC) to bring together black churches to organise non-violent protests against segregation.

He was awarded the Nobel Peace Prize in 1964.

In 1955 he was elected as the chairman of the Montgomery Improvement Association (MIA) and led the Montgomery Bus Boycott, which attracted national attention.

In 1963 he made his famous 'I Have a Dream' speech during a march in Washington.

Martin Luther King was assassinated in 1968 by a white racist called James Earl Ray.

## The impact of the bus boycott

The Montgomery bus boycott made national headlines. Martin Luther King made speeches, gave interviews and appeared on TV. In 1956, a year after Parks' refusal to give up her seat, the Supreme Court ruled that segregated buses were illegal.

### Now try this

What were the causes and effects of the Montgomery bus boycott? List **two causes** and **two effects**.

# Peaceful protest 2

In 1957, Congress passed a Civil Rights Act making it illegal to discriminate against African Americans. The Act was not properly enforced, and the struggle for civil rights continued.

## The Greensboro sit-ins

In February 1960, four black students wanted to be served in a 'whites only' area of the Woolworth department store. When asked to leave, they refused and held a sit-in, staying there until closing. The next day, 25 students joined them. Within 18 months there had been 70 000 sit-ins across the southern states.

Sit-ins were non-violent, and the arrest of peaceful protestors made many white people more sympathetic to the civil rights cause. Stores where sit-ins took place lost money. Some chose to desegregate, but others did not.

## Freedom Riders

The Supreme Court had ordered the desegregation of buses, but African Americans still encountered segregation on public transport. In May 1961, 13 black and white 'Freedom Riders' set out on two buses from Washington DC to highlight the issues.

On 15 May one of the buses was attacked by the KKK and many of the Riders were beaten. They continued to encounter violent attacks, and were often arrested and assaulted by police. Despite this, the Freedom Rides spread, and over 60 took place over the summer of 1961. In November the federal government forced southern states to desegregate their bus facilities.

**The Birmingham Campaign:** Birmingham, Alabama was one of the most segregated cities in America. Throughout spring 1963 Martin Luther King and his followers organised a series of protests there. The protests were peaceful, but King was arrested and police attacked protestors with tear gas, water cannons, dogs and electric batons. Coverage of the attacks caused outrage.

**Further protests**

**Freedom Summer:** A campaign beginning in June 1964 attempted to register as many African-American voters as possible. The campaign encountered violence from the white community, including beatings, drive-by shootings and harassment.

**March on Washington for Jobs and Freedom:** In August 1963 a march took place in Washington DC calling for civil and economic rights for African Americans. Martin Luther King made his famous 'I Have a Dream' speech at the march, which attracted over 200 000 people.

**Selma to Montgomery marches:** Despite the passing of the 1964 Civil Rights Act, African Americans still faced discrimination. In March 1965 non-violent activists marched from Selma to Montgomery. The marches were violently suppressed by police and 3000 people were arrested.

## Key events and legislation after the 1957 Civil Rights Act

**Timeline**

**Feb 1960** Greensboro sit-ins begin and become a common form of non-violent protest.

**Apr 1963** King organises the Birmingham Campaign against segregation; police violently suppress them.

**Aug 1963** King gives his 'I Have a Dream' speech during the March on Washington for Jobs and Freedom.

**June 1964** Volunteers register as many African-American voters as possible in Mississippi, during the Freedom Summer.

**Mar 1965** Selma marches demonstrate African Americans' desire to vote; they encounter violent suppression.

**Aug 1959** Black students are finally allowed into Little Rock High School.

**May 1961** Freedom Riders set out from Washington, DC to show that buses are still segregated.

**May 1963** President Kennedy sends the army to restore order and end segregation in Birmingham.

**Nov 1963** Kennedy, a supporter of the civil rights movement, is assassinated.

**July 1964** President Johnson signs the Civil Rights Act, ending segregation.

**Aug 1965** Voting Rights Act is passed, banning racial discrimination in voting.

**Now try this**

Give **four** ways in which the civil rights activists used non-violent protest in the early 1960s.

# Malcolm X and Black Power

By the mid 1960s the protests led by Martin Luther King had made some progress. However, some African Americans turned to a more radical approach that they called 'Black Power'.

## Black Power

Rejected the slow, non-violent approach – integration meant that African Americans had to fit into a white society that treated them poorly.

Focused on wider issues like poverty, unemployment and the Vietnam War.

Many black Americans became more radical after King's assassination in 1968.

Influenced by the ideas of Malcolm X – demanded rights and improvement for black Americans.

Believed that self-defence was justified – encouraged African Americans to feel pride in their heritage.

The term Black Power was popularised by Stokely Carmichael, a colleague of Martin Luther King.

Symbol was a raised clenched fist.

At the 1968 Mexico Olympics, American medal winners Tommie Smith and John Carlos gave the Black Power salute. They were banned from the team but many young black Americans admired them for making this political statement.

Formed in 1966 – believed that the police force was racist and did not protect African Americans from violence.

Carried weapons and wore a uniform of blue shirts, black trousers, black leather jackets and black berets. Patrolled communities and monitored the behaviour of the police.

**Black Panthers**

Rejected King's call for non-violence – believed that sometimes violence was necessary in self-defence.

Issued a ten-point programme of demands including freedom, employment, education, housing and an end to police brutality against black Americans.

Began social programmes such as breakfast clubs for children and community health clinics.

## Malcolm X (1925–65)

- A troubled upbringing, involved in crime in his youth and spent time in prison.

- Thought non-violent direct action didn't work, because white Americans would never allow African Americans to achieve equality unless by force.

- Initially thought that black Americans should live separately, as white Americans wouldn't allow equality, but later believed integration was possible.

- Encouraged African Americans to take pride in their heritage and fight inequality, with violence if necessary.

- His views influenced Black Power and contrasted King's philosophy of non-violence.

Malcolm X was a member of the Nation of Islam, who believed black Americans should form a Muslim state, separate from white Americans. Malcolm X left the group in 1964 and began to challenge their ideas. He was assassinated by Nation of Islam members in 1965.

## Two Civil Rights Acts

- **The 1964 Civil Rights Act** – banned segregation in schools, supported the right of African Americans to vote, and made racial discrimination illegal.

- **The 1968 Civil Rights Act** – focused on fair housing and protection for civil rights workers. It banned landlords from discriminating against people because of their race or beliefs.

Violations of both acts continued, however after 1968 many Americans saw the battle for civil rights as over. Civil rights groups lost members and funding.

## Now try this

Why did some African Americans reject Martin Luther King's non-violent ideas? Explain your ideas in a short paragraph.

# Kennedy's social policies

John F. Kennedy was elected president in 1960. He had ambitious plans to improve social policies on poverty, education and health, but was assassinated before he could put many of them into action.

## Kennedy's aims

President Kennedy thought that America was on the verge of huge opportunity and dramatic change – he described this as being on the edge of a 'new frontier'. He said that America would need new leaders to cope with new problems and new opportunities.

When Kennedy was elected, he said that he would tackle the problems of inequality, poverty, ill health and poor education so that all Americans could live in dignity. He wanted to encourage Americans to work together to make the country a better place.

When Kennedy used the term 'new frontier', he was making a reference to the original 'American frontier' faced by America's first European settlers. He was suggesting that America was facing the biggest changes since the country was founded.

## The impact of Kennedy's social policies – successes and failures

| Civil rights | Poverty |
|---|---|
| 👍 Gave more government jobs to African Americans. | 👍 Cut taxes to increase the amount of money people had to spend. |
| 👍 Challenged politicians who allowed discrimination. | 👍 Provided funding for employers to create new jobs and train employees. |
| 👍 Created the Commission on Equal Employment Opportunity (CEEO) to make sure federal government didn't discriminate against non-white employees. | 👍 Increased the minimum wage by 25%. |
| | 👍 Amended the Social Security Act (1963) to provide benefits for the unemployed and elderly. |
| 👎 Although Kennedy campaigned for a Civil Rights Act, it was only passed after his death. | 👎 Companies used the funding to buy high-tech equipment and although they trained workers to use it, they also needed fewer staff, so jobs were lost. |
| 👎 Many people thought that this was because Kennedy was too worried about not offending southern politicians who were pro-segregation. | 👎 African Americans were still twice as likely to be unemployed as white Americans. |
| 👎 The CEEO only protected current federal employees – it didn't help African Americans get jobs. | 👎 Minimum wage increases helped people with jobs but didn't make a difference to the unemployed. |
| **Health and housing** | **Education** |
| 👍 Introduced loans of nearly $5 billion to improve housing, clear slums and improve roads and telephone lines. | 👍 Established the Peace Corps, which gave young people an opportunity to travel and learn skills by volunteering abroad. The scheme was a huge success. |
| 👍 Funded development of poor areas. | 👎 Congress blocked his plans to provide federal funding to schools. |
| 👍 Funded research into mental illness. | |
| 👎 Congress blocked Kennedy's plans for Medicare (state provision of healthcare for the elderly). | |
| 👎 People could only take out loans to improve their houses if they could afford repayments, which the poorest people could not. | |

## Now try this

Were Kennedy's social policies a success or a failure? Give at least **three** reasons for your decision.

# Johnson and the 'Great Society'

Lyndon B. Johnson was Kennedy's vice-president. When Kennedy was assassinated in November 1963, Johnson took over as president. Johnson wanted to carry on the work that Kennedy had started and introduced a programme he called the 'Great Society'.

**Poverty:**
- Economic Opportunity Act (1964)
- Food Stamp Act (1964)
- Created the Job Corps to provide free education and training, and the Community Action Program to support volunteer organisations in low-income communities. Established the Food Stamp Program to feed the poorest.

**Key legislation**

**Education:**
- Elementary and Secondary Education Act (1965)
- Higher Education Act (1965)
- Provided significant funding to public schools and universities to help them purchase materials. Established the Head Start Program to ensure proper education, nutrition, and other services for the poorest children.

**Health and Housing:**
- Social Security Act (1965)
- Housing and Urban Development Act (1965)
- Established Medicare to provide health insurance for people over 65, and Medicaid to help provide medical assistance to those on low incomes. Increased funding for housing programmes, and helped the elderly and disabled to pay rent.

Kennedy had tried to win over his opponents using compromise. Johnson had a very different approach. He was an experienced war veteran, and straight-talking Texan who understood southern politicians and wasn't afraid to take them on. He could be manipulative and often poked people in the chest or used his height (he was 1.95 m tall) to intimidate them.

## Johnson's aims

Like Kennedy, Johnson wanted to end poverty and racial discrimination. He believed that America needed to help everyone to reach their potential if the country was going to succeed. He wanted to take action to help that happen, including introducing new **legislation** (laws).

Johnson took over the presidency a year before the 1964 election. His 'Great Society' ideas – and probably some public sympathy after Kennedy's assassination – meant that he won easily.

## Johnson's legacy

| By the end of Johnson's presidency: | However: |
|---|---|
| 👍 226 out of 252 major bills had been passed and government spending on education and health trebled between 1964 and 1967. | 👎 Some people weren't happy with the Great Society agenda, and some resented their taxes being spent on what they saw as government handouts. |
| 👍 Government aid to the poor had nearly trebled since 1960. | 👎 Many thought the government shouldn't be involved in people's lives to this extent. |
| 👍 A million people were retrained under new federal programmes. | 👎 By 1968, unemployment was starting to rise and there were riots in major cities. |
| 👍 2 million children had participated in the Head Start Program. | 👎 Although Johnson's 'Great Society' had lasting impact, many of its programmes were later cut. |
| 👍 The percentage of African Americans living in poverty had fallen to 27% (from 55% in 1960). | 👎 Johnson's social policies were overshadowed by the Vietnam War. He is mainly remembered as the president who took America into a war that resulted in over 58000 American deaths. |

**Now try this**

Who was more successful in improving life for poor Americans, Kennedy or Johnson? Give **at least one** reason for your answer.

 You will need to look at page 33 as well as this one to answer this question.

# Feminist movements

During the 1960s and 1970s a number of feminist movements developed and fought for women's equality. They had an impact on women across America.

Look back at page 24 to remind you what women's lives were like before the Second World War.

## The growth of feminist movements

Women in the 1960s were still not treated equally to men. They were paid less for doing the same work, and many were restricted to largely domestic roles. Television and cinema only depicted women as happy wives and mothers, and sexist institutions such as the Playboy club treated them as little more than objects.

During the 1960s, women fought for equal pay, to get the government to enforce the new anti-discrimination laws, to give women the power to pressure the government and their employers, and to increase women's access to education and professional jobs.

## Women's rights in America

**Timeline**

**1960** Half the workforce are women.

**1961** Kennedy sets up the Presidential Commission on the Status of Women (PCSW).

**1963** PCSW report published; Equal Pay Act.

**1964** Civil Rights Act.

**1966** National Organisation of Women (NOW) founded.

**1972** Equal Rights Amendment (ERA) passed by Congress but fails to become law.

**1973** Roe vs Wade.

## PCSW and the Equal Pay Act

In 1960, President Kennedy set up the Presidential Commission on the Status of Women to investigate the issues faced by women. Its 1963 report found that women:

- earned much less than men for the same work
- were regularly sacked for getting married
- had limited access to education
- faced discrimination at work
- did not have access to proper maternity leave or childcare.

In June 1963, Congress passed the Equal Pay Act, which said that men and women should be paid the same for doing the same work.

## The National Organisation of Women

The 1964 Civil Rights Act banned employers from discriminating on the basis of race or sex. Many women were inspired by the civil rights movement and began to campaign for women's equality. In 1966, NOW was founded. Other groups followed, such as the National Black Feminist Organization. Together these groups were known as the women's movement or the feminist movement.

NOW soon had 40000 members, but most were white and middle class. More radical women formed the 'women's liberation movement', which was sometimes called 'Women's Lib'.

## Roe vs Wade

The women's movement campaigned to legalise abortion, which was banned in many states. They argued that a woman should be able to decide what happened to her own body. In 1969, 'Jane Roe' (not her real name) wanted an abortion and went to court to challenge Henry Wade, the District Attorney of Texas. The case went to the Supreme Court, which ruled in 1973 that women had the right to legal abortion. By then, Jane Roe had had her baby, who was adopted.

## Equal Rights Amendment (ERA)

In 1972, Congress passed an amendment to the Constitution that would give women equal rights with men. However, a campaign against the ERA, led by a woman called Phyllis Schlafly, argued that it would cause 'undesirable' consequences such as women in combat, gay marriage and unisex toilets. Schlafly's campaign was a success – the ERA did not become law because it was not supported by enough states.

**Now try this**

Give **two** examples of the impact of feminist movements on the lives of women in the 1960s and early 1970s.

# Exam overview

This page introduces you to the main features and requirements of the Paper 1 Section A exam paper for America, 1920–1973: Opportunity and inequality.

## About Paper 1

- Paper 1 is for your period study and your wider world depth study.
- Section A of the paper will be on your period study, which is America, 1920–1973: Opportunity and inequality.
- You must answer **all** questions in Section A.
- You will receive two documents: a question paper which will contain the questions and interpretations, and an answer booklet.

Here we are focusing on Section A and your period study. However, the same exam paper will also include Section B, where you will answer questions about your wider world depth study.

The Paper 1 exam lasts for 1 hour 45 minutes (105 minutes). There are 84 marks in total: **40 marks for Section A;** 40 marks, plus 4 marks for spelling, punctuation and grammar, for Section B. You should spend approximately **50 minutes on Section A** and 50 minutes on Section B with 5 minutes to check your answers.

## The questions

The questions for Paper 1 Section A will always follow this pattern:

You can see examples of all six questions on pages 39–44, and in the practice questions on pages 46–54.

**Question 1**
How does **Interpretation B** differ from **Interpretation A** about …?
Explain your answer using **Interpretations A and B**.
           **(4 marks)**

Question 1 targets AO4. AO4 is about analysing, evaluating and making substantiated judgements. Spend about 5 minutes on this question, which is about **the ways in which the interpretations differ.**

**Question 2**
Why might the authors of **Interpretations A and B** have a different interpretation about …?
Explain your answer using **Interpretations A and B** and your contextual knowledge.    **(4 marks)**

Question 2 also targets AO4. Spend about 5 minutes on this question which is about **suggesting and explaining why** the interpretations differ.

**Question 3**
Which interpretation do you find more convincing about …?
Explain your answer using **Interpretations A and B** and your contextual knowledge.    **(8 marks)**

Question 3 also targets AO4. You should spend approximately 10 minutes on this question, which is about **evaluating** the interpretations.

**Question 4**
Describe two …          **(4 marks)**

Question 4 targets AO1. AO1 is about showing your knowledge and understanding of the **key features and characteristics** of the topic. Spend about 5 minutes on this question.

**Question 5**
In what ways …?
Explain your answer.        **(8 marks)**

Question 5 targets both AO1 and AO2. AO2 is about explaining and analysing historical events using historical concepts, such as causation, consequence, change, continuity, similarity and difference. Spend about 10 minutes on this question, which focuses on **change: explaining how a group or development was affected by something.**

**Question 6**
Which of the following was the more important reason why …?
(Two bullet points)
Explain your answer with reference to both bullet points.       **(12 marks)**

Question 6 also targets both AO1 and AO2. Spend about 15 minutes on this question, which is about making a judgement and focuses on **causation, consequence, change and/or continuity.**

# Interpretation skills

This exam asks you to analyse, evaluate and make judgements about interpretations.

## What are interpretations?

For the first three questions in the exam paper you will be asked to study two different **interpretations** of a particular enquiry or event. Interpretations are compiled after the time period or event. Interpretations can be accounts of events written by people who were there or written by historians. They might also be images, such as reconstructive drawings or diagrams of events. All interpretations will contain people's views and opinions.

As well as analysing interpretations, you will need to evaluate them and make judgements about them. In all cases, you need to keep the **historical context** in mind.

## Analysing interpretations

When analysing interpretations you need to try and work out the **message** of the interpretation. Do this separately for each interpretation and then compare them. You then need to think about the following for the exam questions:

- **how** they differ (question 1)
- **why** they differ (question 2)
- which interpretation is **more convincing** (question 3).

Look at each interpretation carefully. Underline information or annotate the interpretation with your ideas to help you identify key points that you can use in your answer.

## Contextual knowledge

Questions 2 and 3 will both ask you to explain your answer using the interpretations and your **contextual knowledge**. This means that you need to think about what you know about the event or development and how the interpretations fit with what you know. Only use knowledge that's relevant to the topic in the question and that is linked to what is discussed in the interpretation itself.

As you consider each interpretation, ask yourself: What do I know about these events/developments? How is this reflected in the interpretation? How is this linked to the focus of the question?

## Provenance

Before both interpretations in the exam paper you will be given several lines of **provenance**. This will vary for each but is likely to include some details about the author and their work or experiences, and when their work was published. This information is as important as the interpretation itself as it will help you establish the **purpose** of the interpretation, which will help you in questions 2 and 3 in particular.

**Provenance** means where something comes from — where it started or came into existence.

## Hints and tips for analysing and evaluating interpretations

| How complete? | How objective? | What is the chosen emphasis? |
|---|---|---|
| The interpretations can be different because they are concerned with finding out about different aspects of the enquiry and may cover different ground. Sometimes, historians set out to look at one aspect specifically, whereas others may want to look at related issues in a broader sense. | Historians can hold different views because they come from a particular school of thought. Therefore, their questions and answers are shaped by their wider views of society and how it works and has worked in the past. This can have an important impact on the judgements and opinions they hold about historical matters. | Sometimes, historians use the same sources but reach different views because they place a different level of importance on the same evidence. They may have access to the same material sources as each other, but will draw different conclusions about the significance of that evidence. |

# Interpretations A and B

These interpretations are referred to in the worked examples on pages 39–41.

**SECTION A**

**America, 1920–1973: Opportunity and inequality**

Read **Interpretations A** and **B** and answer questions 1, 2 and 3 on pages 39, 40 and 41.

**Interpretation A** From an article by S.B. Fuller in 1980.
S.B Fuller (1905–88) was a self-made businessman – he had become successful as a result of his own efforts – and a prominent Republican.

For each interpretation you will be given short details on the work the interpretation comes from. In this case, who wrote the article, and when.

You will be given a few lines of information about the author and/or the interpretation. In this case you are told that the person who wrote the article was a Republican businessman.

The New Deal of Franklin Roosevelt hurt us. He was a rich man's son. All he received was given to him. So he thinks it's right to give. He didn't understand, when you give to people, you hurt them. We had soup lines and the Depression because men lost confidence in themselves. … A dog you feed will not hunt. If you want a dog that hunts, you have to let him get hungry. … You're free to eat if you pay for your food, and you are free to starve if you don't get the equivalent to pay for it.

For each interpretation, underline or highlight any important words or phrases and annotate them.

**Interpretation B** From a book called *Freedom From Fear: The American People in Depression and War, 1929–1945*, written by David M. Kennedy and published in 1999.
David M. Kennedy is an American historian who specialises in American history. This book won the Pulitzer Prize for history in 2000.
Frances Perkins was Roosevelt's Secretary of Labor.

… what needs emphasis, in the final accounting, is not what the New Deal failed to do but how it managed to do so much in … the mid-1930s. That brief span of years, it is now clear, constituted one of only a handful of episodes in American history when substantial and lasting social change has occurred—when the country was, in measurable degree, remade ... Franklin Roosevelt's social vision was clear enough. 'We are going to make a country,' he once said to Frances Perkins, 'in which no one is left out.'

It's a good idea to compare and contrast the provenance of the two interpretations. Why might the authors have a different view? Are they looking at different things? At different times? In different ways?

Your annotations on the interpretation could also include any points that contrast with the other interpretation.

# Question 1: Explaining how interpretations differ

Question 1 on your exam paper will ask you to identify differences in two interpretations: 'What is the main difference between the views ...'. There are 4 marks available for this question.

## Worked example

**Read Interpretations A and B on page 38.**

How does **Interpretation B** differ from **Interpretation A** about the effects of the New Deal?

Explain your answer, using **Interpretations A and B**.

**(4 marks)**

Remember to include points from **both** interpretations. It's important to refer directly to the interpretations and include short quotations to support what you say.

**Links** You can revise the New Deal on pages 18–21.

## How interpretations differ

In a question that asks **how** one interpretation differs from another, you need to analyse both interpretations and explain how they are different. Look for the important or key differences, not just surface details. A fundamental difference might be that they believe different factors are more important for explaining why something happened. A surface detail would just repeat content from the interpretations without explaining how they are different. You don't need to explain why they are different, as you will do this in question 2.

## Sample answer

The interpretations are different because one focuses on Roosevelt being a rich man's son who gave other people's money away, and the other thinks that Roosevelt created lasting social change.

This answer focuses on a difference in surface details. Instead, you need to make sure you look for key, underlying differences in the interpretations.

## Improved answer

In Interpretation A, Fuller claims that Roosevelt's social plans were caused by the fact that he was protected by a rich family and did not have to make his own way in the world. He describes the idea that giving people too much help weakens them.

In contrast, Kennedy argues in Interpretation B that the New Deal led to 'substantial and lasting social change' within a short period of time. This indicates that the authors have different ideas about Roosevelt's motivations, and about the impact of the New Deal. Fuller claims Roosevelt's weakness caused people to become dependent and worsened the Depression while Kennedy believes Roosevelt's strength helped America to overcome the Depression within a 'brief span of years'.

Use short quotations to support your analysis.

Make sure you focus on the key point of difference, rather than on more minor differences. Here the student does this well by picking out that Interpretation A claims the New Deal worsened the effects of the Depression by encouraging people to depend on the government, while Interpretation B says that Roosevelt 'remade' the country and caused major social change.

You need to identify and explain a key difference, and support it with detailed points from **both** interpretations.

Think about the specific language you use in your answer, such as: 'argues', 'claims', 'states' and 'backs this up'. These phrases help you to produce a better answer because they help show you are analysing another person's judgement or opinion about something.

# Question 2: Explaining why interpretations differ

Question 2 on your exam paper will ask you to explain why two interpretations give different views. There are 4 marks available for this question.

## Worked example

Why might the authors of **Interpretations A** and **B** on page 38 have a different interpretation about the impact of the New Deal?

Explain your answer using **Interpretations A** and **B** and your contextual knowledge.     **(4 marks)**

Remember: you **must** include your own contextual knowledge in your answer.

### 'Why' questions

In a question that asks you why authors have different interpretations, you need to offer and explain an idea about **why** there are differences. You need to show you understand that historical interpretations are judgements and opinions based on evidence, and that, as such, different views can exist.

**Links** You can revise the New Deal on pages 18–21.

## Sample answer

The two interpretations differ mainly because the authors are writing for different purposes. In Interpretation A, Fuller is describing his own experience, while in Interpretation B, Kennedy is writing an academic text.

Fuller argues Roosevelt's New Deal was the result of his own experience of being part of a rich family and not understanding how ordinary people act. He thinks that this meant that the New Deal caused harm. In contrast, Kennedy says that the New Deal had a positive impact and 'remade' the country to be fairer. I think the authors have different ideas about the role of government. Fuller believes in individualism while Kennedy argues the New Deal happened because voters had rejected individualism.

Starting your answer with a basic explanation of the differences – in this case the purpose of each interpretation – is a good idea. Then you should go on to to give a deeper explanation.

You must always read the **provenance** of the interpretations carefully, as this student obviously has, as this will give you important clues about their focus and the evidence used.

You could try to take into account the **context** of why the interpretations were written, explaining why there are differences.

As the student has done here you must try to make the explanation as clear as possible and you must refer to **both** interpretations.

# Question 3: Evaluating interpretations

Question 3 on your exam paper will ask you to evaluate two interpretations by asking which interpretation you find more convincing. There are 8 marks available for this question.

## Worked example

Which interpretation do you find more convincing about the impact of the New Deal?

Explain your answer using **Interpretations A** and **B** on page 38 and your contextual knowledge. **(8 marks)**

### Which is more convincing?

You must:

- ✓ explore different views on the debate
- ✓ reach a clear **judgement** yourself
- ✓ give detailed knowledge of the **context** and wider issues
- ✓ use **both** interpretations – don't just rely on one.

### Sample extract

I think Kennedy's interpretation is more convincing than Fuller's. Fuller seems to mix up the causes of the Depression with Roosevelt's policies to deal with it. Kennedy accepts there were some failures, but still thinks that Roosevelt made positive changes.

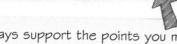 **Links** You can revise the New Deal on pages 18–21.

Remember: you **must** include your own contextual knowledge in your answer.

Give your opinion clearly as this student has done.

Always support the points you make with evidence from the source and your own knowledge – the student doesn't do this here.

### Improved extract

Fuller claims that the New Deal caused people to lose confidence in themselves, and then suggests that it was the loss of confidence that caused the soup lines during the Depression. However, the Depression began under Hoover's government that preached 'rugged individualism', so Fuller's argument seems confused and I find it difficult to agree with it. Fuller was a prominent Republican and had started his own successful businesses, which will have affected his view of Roosevelt's social programmes. His powerful language comparing men to dogs that need to be kept hungry so they will hunt appears cruel, but it reminds me of Hoover's arguments for individualism.

Kennedy's interpretation is more balanced. It acknowledges that America was not functioning effectively during this period, and that the New Deal did not achieve everything that Roosevelt intended, but he also argues Roosevelt made 'substantial and lasting social change'. This is supported by a study of the period, as the New Deal certainly had a lasting impact on America.

You could highlight key points in the interpretations themselves to help you focus on the precise arguments that you need to evaluate in order to make your judgement.

This answer engages directly with the claims made in **both** interpretations.

You need to put both interpretations into **context** as the student has done here by bringing in their own knowledge of the Depression and the New Deal.

# Question 4: Describing features or characteristics

Question 4 on your exam paper will ask you to describe two features or characteristics of America 1920–1973. There are 4 marks available for this question.

## Worked example

Describe two problems caused by the policy of prohibition between 1920 and 1933. **(4 marks)**

### Sample answer

Prohibition did not work because people could get alcohol from speakeasies. Gangsters were involved in selling alcohol and this created more problems such as addiction and alcohol poisoning, corruption and violent activity.

### What does 'describe' mean?

**Describe** means give an account of the main characteristics of something. You should develop your description with relevant details to show that you understand them. However, you do not need to include reasons or justifications.

🔗 **Links** You can revise prohibition on page 8.

Make sure you only give two problems and that you describe each one with some detail. This answer lists four problems (gangster involvement, addiction and alcohol poisoning, corruption, and violence) but gives little detail about any of them.

Read the question carefully. This question asks for problems caused by prohibition, but the student seems to be answering a question about whether or not it was effective.

### Improved answer

One of the problems caused by prohibition was worsening social problems. The argument for banning alcohol was that it would make America a better, healthier country, but instead social problems increased, as shown by the rise in addiction and alcohol poisoning, and arrests for disorder and drink-driving.

Another problem was the increase in criminal activity associated with the sale and transportation of alcohol. The lack of legal access to alcohol meant that 'speakeasies' were used by large numbers of people. This profitable market made gangsters a lot of money and contributed to the power of organised crime.

It's a good idea to separate your two problems in different paragraphs as the student has done here. This shows clearly that you have identified two separate problems.

You need to give **supporting detail** for each problem, as the student has done here.

# Question 5: Explaining change

Question 5 on your exam paper will ask you to explain how a group or development was affected by something. There are 8 marks available for this question.

## Worked example

In what ways were the lives of African Americans affected by the civil rights movement?

Explain your answer. **(8 marks)**

### Sample extract

Before the civil rights movement, segregation affected the lives of African Americans by controlling their everyday lives.

Although African Americans were technically free after the abolition of slavery, the white minority in the southern states passed the Jim Crow Laws, which said that African Americans couldn't use the same shops, hotels, restaurants and taxis as white people. They could be made to give up their seats to white people on buses, and were only allowed to live in less desirable areas. There were restrictions that were intended to stop African Americans from voting.

Organisations such as the NAACP were set up to campaign for the end of segregation, equal access to voting, housing and education, and an end to discrimination in employment. The fight for civil rights was led by individuals who had been treated unfairly by the Jim Crow laws and who protested publicly about their treatment with the support of groups such as the NAACP. These protests helped to change public opinion and increase support for further challenges to segregation. The NAACP organised the registration of African-American children at white schools, resulting in the legal challenge of Brown vs Board of Education of Topeka which ended with a 1954 Supreme Court ruling that segregation in public schools was unconstitutional. The legal victory set the precedent to start the removal of other Jim Crow laws.

Another example was when Rosa Parks was arrested when she refused to give up her seat on a bus. Martin Luther King and the NAACP used Parks' case to encourage the 1955 Montgomery Bus Boycott, which eventually ended segregation on the city's buses.

### Explaining 'in what ways'

This question requires you to describe and explain how and why a group or development **changed**. There will always be a number of different ways in which change happened. The best answers will also show that change was not the same for everyone or everything.

 **Links** You can revise segregation on pages 12, and 29–32.

It's a good idea to show how something was different from before. For example, here the student explains that before the civil rights movement, African Americans lived under segregation.

The impact of segregation is explained further in this paragraph, giving context for the rest of the answer.

Try to explain the **reasons** for the changes that took place. In this case, the student points out that organisations were formed to fight segregation and that important individuals organised successful protests.

Give an example of **change.** This answer describes how African Americans began to protest and what happened as a result. Support your example with details. Here the student gives examples of protests and how they brought about change.

# Question 6: Making a judgement

Question 6 on your exam paper will identify two reasons for you and ask you to analyse them. You will need to decide which was the more important reason why something did or did not happen. There are 12 marks available for this question.

## Worked example

Which of the following was the more important reason why women gained greater equality with men in the years 1945–73?

- The Second World War
- The feminist movement

Explain your answer with reference to both bullet points.

**(12 marks)**

## Sample extract

The Second World War was the most important reason for the move towards women's equality in the period 1945–73. The feminist movement was able to gain power, focus and support because of the impact the Second World War had on women's lives.

The Second World War created employment opportunities for women, which gave them economic power and independence. 350000 women joined the armed forces, and many more took over men's jobs in factories, shipyards and railways. By the end of the war, women made up a third of America's workforce. This made women more visible and meant that they took a more active role in public life now that they were no longer confined to the home. Women's contribution to the war effort earned them respect and helped the campaign for women's equality.

Once women were part of the workplace, they were able to see that their work was as valuable as men's, and this meant that they were more inclined to fight for equal pay. Women became more likely to support groups such as the National Organisation of Women and other organisations campaigning for women's equality.

### The balance of Assessment Objectives

Question 6 is an essay question which is worth 12 marks in total. Of this, 6 marks are for AO1 and 6 marks are for AO2. Therefore you need to combine information and understanding (AO1) equally with analysis and explanation (AO2) for the best results. You also need to reach a judgement and follow a sustained line of reasoning which is coherent, relevant, substantiated and logically structured.

🔗 **Links** You can revise the Second World War on pages 23–24 and the feminist movement on page 35.

Begin your answer with a strong opening paragraph. This should lay out **your opinions** of the reasons given in the question and, most importantly, come to a **judgement** about which reason was more important.

You **must** explain **both** reasons given in the bullet points giving detailed information on what happened and why.

Only focus on the reasons given in the bullet points in the question, as the student has done here. You don't need to include any other reasons in your answer.

Make sure you show how the reasons are **connected.** Here, the student points out that women's role in the war helped the fight for equal pay by the feminist movement.

This is an extract from a student's answer. In a full answer, you would need to go on to discuss the contributions of the feminist movement, such as the 1963 Equal Pay Act and Roe vs Wade. You would then need to finish with a conclusion setting out why the Second World War was more important, referring to both bullet points.

# Practice

You will need to refer to the interpretations below in your answers to questions 1, 2 and 3 on pages 46–48.

---

### SECTION A

### America, 1920–1973: Opportunity and inequality

Answer **all six questions** on pages 46 to 53.

Read **Interpretations A** and **B** and answer the questions **1, 2** and **3** on pages 46 to 48.

**Interpretation A**   From an Interview with Bobby Seale in 1988.
Bobby Seale was one of the founding members of the Black
Panther organisation.

> … If you push a panther into a corner, if he can't go left and he can't go right, he
> will tend to come out of that corner to wipe out its aggressor, whoever had pushed
> it into the corner. And the analogy[1] was that's where Black people been pushed.
> Peaceful demonstrators exercised the first amendment of the Constitution[2] of the
> United States and … racists brutaliz[ed] them: they couldn't go left, couldn't go right.

[1]**analogy**: comparison
[2]**first amendment of the Constitution**: this protects the freedom of speech,
religion and the press, as well as the right to peaceful protest

**Interpretation B**   Chris Simkins in his article 'Non-violence Was Key to Civil Rights Movement',
published on the Voice of America website in 2004. Voice of America is a
government-funded radio station that broadcasts outside the USA.
Chris Simkins is an American TV journalist who produced a highly praised
documentary about the civil rights movement.

> A major factor in the success of the movement was the strategy of protesting for
> equal rights without using violence. Civil rights leader Rev. Martin Luther King
> championed this approach as an alternative to armed uprising. King's non-violent
> movement was inspired by the teachings of Indian leader Mahatma Gandhi.
>
> Led by King, millions of black people took to the streets for peaceful protests as
> well as acts of civil disobedience and economic boycotts in what some leaders
> describe as America's second civil war.

# Practice

Put your skills and knowledge into practice with the following question. You will need to refer to Interpretations A and B on page 45 in your answer.

1  How does **Interpretation B** differ from **Interpretation A** about the effectiveness of non-violence in the campaign for civil rights in America?

Explain your answer, using **Interpretations A** and **B**.

**(4 marks)**

Guided  Interpretations A and B both discuss the tactics

used by African Americans in the campaign for civil rights

in America.

...........................................................................................

...........................................................................................

...........................................................................................

...........................................................................................

...........................................................................................

...........................................................................................

...........................................................................................

...........................................................................................

...........................................................................................

...........................................................................................

...........................................................................................

...........................................................................................

...........................................................................................

...........................................................................................

...........................................................................................

...........................................................................................

...........................................................................................

...........................................................................................

You have 1 hour 45 minutes for the **whole** of Paper 1 which means you have **50 minutes** for **Section A**. You should use the time carefully to answer all the questions fully. In the exam, remember to leave 5 minutes or so to check your work when you've finished both Sections A and B.

Links  You can revise the civil rights movement on pages 29–32.

You can revise how to evaluate interpretations on page 37.

Spend about **5 minutes** on this answer. You need to identify the **key difference**, rather than just surface differences.

Make sure you refer to the content of **both** interpretations.

Remember to use specific words and phrases in your answer such as: 'argues', 'claims', 'states' and 'backs this up'. These help show you are analysing another person's judgement or opinion.

It's a good idea to use short **quotations** from the interpretations to support your answer.

Remember you don't need to explain **why** the interpretations are different.

# Practice

Put your skills and knowledge into practice with the following question. You will need to refer to Interpretations A and B on page 45 in your answer.

2  Why might the authors of **Interpretations A** and **B** have a different interpretation about the effectiveness of non-violence in the campaign for civil rights in America?

Explain your answer using **Interpretations A** and **B** and your contextual knowledge.                    (4 marks)

........................................................................................

........................................................................................

........................................................................................

........................................................................................

........................................................................................

........................................................................................

........................................................................................

........................................................................................

........................................................................................

........................................................................................

........................................................................................

........................................................................................

........................................................................................

........................................................................................

........................................................................................

........................................................................................

........................................................................................

........................................................................................

........................................................................................

You should spend about **5 minutes** on this answer.

You can revise how to evaluate interpretations on page 37.

**Links** You can revise the campaign for civil rights on pages 29–32.

Remember that the **provenance** information given before each interpretation will help you with this question.

It is essential to use your **own contextual knowledge** in answering this question.

A good way of answering this specific question is to think about the **purpose** of each interpretation.

Make sure you refer to **both** the interpretations to support your answer.

# Practice

Put your skills and knowledge into practice with the following question. You will need to refer to Interpretations A and B on page 45 in your answer.

3   Which interpretation do you find more convincing about the effectiveness of non-violence in the campaign for civil rights in America?

Explain your answer using **Interpretations A** and **B** and your contextual knowledge.                    **(8 marks)**

**Guided**   I find Interpretation ............ more convincing because

...........................................................................................

...........................................................................................

...........................................................................................

...........................................................................................

...........................................................................................

...........................................................................................

...........................................................................................

...........................................................................................

...........................................................................................

...........................................................................................

...........................................................................................

...........................................................................................

...........................................................................................

...........................................................................................

...........................................................................................

...........................................................................................

...........................................................................................

...........................................................................................

...........................................................................................

...........................................................................................

...........................................................................................

...........................................................................................

You should spend about 10 minutes on this question.

You can revise how to analyse interpretations on page 37.

Say which interpretation you find more convincing in the opening sentence: A or B.

**Links** You can revise the campaign for civil rights on pages 29–32.

Start with a clear **judgement** about which interpretation you think is more convincing. You could also include reasons why the other interpretation is less convincing at this stage.

It's essential to refer to **both** interpretations throughout your answer.

Remember to include your own knowledge of the **context** – about how different groups attempted to achieve racial equality.

You should build an argument throughout your answer, giving a number of reasons why one interpretation is more convincing and the other one less convincing.

# Practice

Use this page to continue your answer to question 3.

........................................................................

........................................................................

........................................................................

........................................................................

........................................................................

........................................................................

........................................................................

........................................................................

........................................................................

........................................................................

........................................................................

........................................................................

........................................................................

........................................................................

It doesn't really matter which Interpretation you find more convincing – there isn't a 'correct' answer as it's just your own opinion. What's important is to explain **why** you think that particular interpretation is more convincing and support your reasons with **evidence** from your contextual knowledge.

# Practice

Put your skills and knowledge into practice with the following question.

**4** Describe **two** problems faced by American society during the 1920s. **(4 marks)**

..............................................................................................

..............................................................................................

..............................................................................................

..............................................................................................

..............................................................................................

..............................................................................................

..............................................................................................

..............................................................................................

..............................................................................................

..............................................................................................

..............................................................................................

..............................................................................................

..............................................................................................

..............................................................................................

..............................................................................................

..............................................................................................

..............................................................................................

..............................................................................................

You should spend about 5 minutes on this question.

**Links** You can revise the impact of the Second World War on pages 23–24.

Only describe **two** problems. You won't receive any credit for describing more than two and will waste valuable time if you do.

Write a separate paragraph for each of your two problems. This will show you have identified two different problems.

You need to include some **details** for each problem. This will show that you understand **how** it was a problem.

# Practice

Put your skills and knowledge into practice with the following question.

5  In what ways did the lives of women in America change in the 1920s?

Explain your answer.                                    **(8 marks)**

.......................................................................................................

.......................................................................................................

.......................................................................................................

.......................................................................................................

.......................................................................................................

.......................................................................................................

.......................................................................................................

.......................................................................................................

.......................................................................................................

.......................................................................................................

.......................................................................................................

.......................................................................................................

.......................................................................................................

.......................................................................................................

.......................................................................................................

.......................................................................................................

.......................................................................................................

.......................................................................................................

.......................................................................................................

.......................................................................................................

.......................................................................................................

.......................................................................................................

You should spend about 10 minutes on this question.

**Links** You can revise the position of women in the 1920s on page 7.

You need to identify the **changes** in people's lives. Remember to include a number of different ways in which women's lives changed.

Each example of change you describe must be supported with **detail**.

Remember to explain how the change was **different** from before. For example, before the First World War, American women had few opportunities. Very few women worked. During the war, women began to work and this gave them economic freedom. By 1929, around 10 million women had jobs.

You could include examples from a variety of different things such as employment, fashion, social conventions and the increasing divorce rate.

# Practice

Use this page to continue your answer to question 5.

..................................................................

..................................................................

..................................................................

..................................................................

..................................................................

..................................................................

..................................................................

..................................................................

..................................................................

..................................................................

..................................................................

..................................................................

..................................................................

..................................................................

..................................................................

For each change you describe, try to explain the **reason** why this change happened. For example, more women began to work during the First World War because many men had joined the armed forces.

# Practice

Put your skills and knowledge into practice with the following question.

6  Which of the following elements of Roosevelt's New Deal of 1932 had the biggest impact on America?

- Social change
- Economic policy

Explain your answer with reference to both bullet points.

**(12 marks)**

You should spend about 15 minutes on this question.

 **Links** You can revise the New Deal on pages 18–21.

**Guided**  The New Deal had important economic and social effects. However, I think the element that had the most impact was

In your opening paragraph, come to a **judgement** about which reason was more important.

Remember that you need to concentrate equally on giving information to show what you know about the events in the bullet points **and** analysing and explaining how they contributed to the impact of the New Deal.

Examine **both** of the bullet points given in the question and give detailed information on both of them throughout your answer.

You don't need to include any other reasons besides those given in the bullet points. You just need to **evaluate** the two given reasons.

# Practice

Use this page to continue your answer to question 6.

...................................................................

...................................................................

...................................................................

...................................................................

...................................................................

...................................................................

...................................................................

...................................................................

...................................................................

...................................................................

...................................................................

...................................................................

...................................................................

...................................................................

...................................................................

...................................................................

...................................................................

...................................................................

...................................................................

...................................................................

...................................................................

...................................................................

...................................................................

...................................................................

...................................................................

...................................................................

...................................................................

If possible, you should also show how the two reasons given in the bullet points are **connected** to each other, for example that economic changes often had social impacts or vice versa. You could mention that the end of prohibition (a social change) allowed the government to raise money through taxation (economic impact).

Try to build an argument throughout the whole essay.

Use this page to continue your answer to question 6.

# ANSWERS

*Where an exemplar answer is given, this is not necessarily the only correct response. In most cases there is a range of responses that can gain full marks.*

## SUBJECT CONTENT

## American people and the boom

### 1. The American people

For example, two from:
* Tensions between different races.
* An imbalance in power and influence leading to inequality.
* Differences in wealth leading to poverty and resentment.

### 2. Causes of the boom

Any three from:
* The access to credit agreements through hire purchase and more disposable income from higher wages allowed ordinary people to buy goods that would have been unaffordable before.
* Advertising helped create and drive demand for goods and services that had been inaccessible for ordinary people before.
* The growth in the country's economic resources allowed ordinary people to use new technology such as fridges and record players.
* Making new consumer products created jobs, which meant that workers had disposable income to buy more products.

### 3. Ford and the motor industry

Mass production was very fast. It used the assembly line process, with skilled workers who could focus on a specific part of production. As a result, the cost of the final product fell dramatically and made cars more accessible to ordinary people. The demand for cars increased demand for the raw materials such as glass, leather and steel. This created even more jobs and more disposable income in the economy. As more people drove, more roadside restaurants and hotels opened. Houses were built in the city suburbs because people could now drive to work.

### 4. Inequalities of wealth

Companies were focused on making profits and this kept wages low for low-skilled and unskilled workers. These groups were also affected by the changing demand for products, which reduced demand for traditional goods such as coal and cotton. This changing demand meant that more people who had previously had stable employment as skilled workers entered the unskilled job market. This added competition and also kept wages low. Ethnic minorities faced additional problems. Native Americans were moved to reservations where they could no longer live their traditional way of life, and were given the worst land, which made it hard to grow crops. African Americans often worked as labourers and sharecroppers on rented land where living conditions were awful.

### 5. The stock market boom

One from the following:
* The lack of government regulation of the stock market meant that a lot of money was invested in companies that did not make anything. This meant that lots of people owned shares that were not attached to any real value.
* The relaxation of lending rules with the banks led to a large amount of borrowing by businesses and ordinary people. Many people used borrowed money to buy shares, which was very risky.

### 6. Entertainment

The 1920s was a time of economic growth and changes in employment, and this led to an increase in leisure time and disposable income. People could afford to go out to the cinema or a sports game, and businesses created products for people to spend money on. Advertising and media also played an important role. They spread ideas about new activities and crazes to many different people and communities.

### 7. Women in society

For example, two from:
* The financial independence some women achieved during the First World War gave them choices they hadn't had before.
* Women had the option of choosing to live alone. The number of women divorcing their husbands doubled.
* Women were not as restricted by social rules and were able to choose to dress and act differently, leading to the 'flappers'.

### 8. Prohibition

For example, any two from:
* People wanted to drink, giving many a reason to break the law.
* It was very difficult to stop alcohol being smuggled into the USA.
* The money made from smuggling and selling alcohol meant that gangsters could bribe police and judges.

### 9. Organised crime

Any two from:
* His 'Robin Hood' persona gave him protection through fame and linked him with celebrities and charities.
* He forged protective relationships with law enforcement officers, which sheltered him from some legal investigation.
* The lack of willing witnesses to Capone's crimes made it difficult to convict him of his Mafia crimes.

### 10. The experiences of immigrants

I came to America from the south of Italy. My family is very poor and I came to America because I believed I would have a better life. I heard stories about how anyone who would work hard could become wealthy – but it isn't always true. I work very hard but I am still poor. Lots of Americans don't like immigrants and pay us less or refuse to employ us at all.

## 11. The impact of immigration

Any two from:

- The opportunities in America were not easily available to all, leaving many working for very low wages and living in awful housing.
- The growing hostility facing new immigrants to America from native-born citizens must have made life more difficult, and contributed to making integration harder.
- Many immigrants did not speak very much English and stayed within their own communities, making it more difficult to learn the language and integrate into society.

## 12. Experiences of African Americans

Racial discrimination was caused by a belief that white people were superior to people of colour. Access to basic rights depended on skin colour, which caused society to divide along racial lines.

## 13. The Ku Klux Klan

For example, one of:

- The KKK included people with political and legal power. This gave protection to other members to engage in violent and illegal activities, and meant that black people were not protected by the law.
- As KKK practices were secret it meant that African Americans could not be sure who was a member. Every white person was therefore a potential enemy.

## 14. The Red Scare

The case against them was very weak. They were targeted because they were anarchists. The judge was biased so they didn't get a fair trial.

# Bust – Americans' experiences of the Depression and New Deal

## 15. The Wall Street Crash

Answers should include at least two of the following points:

- People lost money as the value of their shares dropped.
- People couldn't repay the loans they had taken out to buy shares.
- People lost their life savings when banks failed and many people and businesses lost everything.
- It was harder for people and businesses to borrow money.
- Many people lost their jobs as businesses closed.
- People had less money to spend and found it hard to buy food and pay rent.

## 16. The Great Depression: impact

There are several acceptable answers, as long as you provide evidence to support your ideas. For example:

I think farmers were most affected by the Depression. Farmers and farmworkers lost their livelihoods and farmers often had to sell their farms due to their debts and falling prices for their produce. Those living in the Dust Bowl lost everything and had to try to find labouring work elsewhere.

## 17. Hoover's response

Hoover's belief in individualism was a key part of his personal and political position – he truly thought that the government should not get involved because providing direct relief would stop people being able to help themselves. He put a stop to policies that would have provided direct help to people who were facing unemployment and poverty.

This belief in individualism and laissez-faire meant that the measures Hoover introduced were quite limited, and many of them had unwanted consequences. For example, the Smoot–Hawley Tariff Act was meant to increase demand for American goods, but instead it caused other governments to stop imports of American products.

## 18. Roosevelt becomes president

You can argue the case either way here, as long as you support your answer with evidence.
For example:

**Hoover lost the 1932 election**, because the impact of the Depression meant that voters were angry that the government wasn't doing more to support them. Roosevelt's New Deal was a reaction to Hoover's unpopular policies. Despite his unpopularity, Hoover refused to change his position, which angered voters. Hoover's opposition to repealing prohibition was also a huge mistake as this won Roosevelt a lot of support.

**Roosevelt won the 1932 election**, because although Hoover's policies were unpopular, that wasn't enough on its own. In order to win, Roosevelt offered the American people a believable alternative. Roosevelt presented himself as the right man for the job, and ran a very strong campaign using public appearances all over the country and a campaign theme tune. He was a gifted public speaker and made good use of this by making up to 15 speeches a day. However unpopular Hoover was, to win by such a landslide Roosevelt must have been more than just 'not Hoover'.

You could also argue that the result of the 1932 election was a combination of both Hoover's unpopularity and Roosevelt's policies and clever campaigning.

## 19. The start of the New Deal

You can argue that any one of the three main actions was the most significant as long as you give reasons for your choice. For example:

- **The Economy Act** was the most significant in the first 100 days, because it quickly raised money to pay for New Deal programmes. This created jobs and provided aid, which helped to stabilise the economy and relieve poverty.
- **The Emergency Banking Act** was the most significant because it restored people's trust in the banking system, and ended the panic that had made normal banking impossible. It also gave the banks a billion dollars they could lend to businesses, and got rid of corrupt and badly run banks, preventing future problems.
- **The Beer Act** was the most significant because it ended prohibition and reduced the influence of organised crime. It also created jobs and tax income from alcohol sales.

## 20. Opposition to the New Deal

Lots of very powerful people did not like the New Deal – rich people resented high taxes, Republican politicians thought it intruded too much on people's lives, and the Supreme Court ruled that parts of it were unconstitutional. These people expressed their criticism very clearly, but it made little difference because most ordinary people were in favour of the help the New Deal gave them.

## 21. Evaluating Roosevelt's New Deal

Reasons why the New Deal was a success, any two from:

- The protection of workers' rights and the minimum wage gave security to people who were very worried about being able to support themselves and their families.

- The Social Security Act provided a safety net for those people who were without a job while jobs were being created.
- GNP rose dramatically.
- The number of bank failures went down.

Reasons why the New Deal was not a success, any two from:
- Although it created jobs, it did not solve the problem of unemployment completely.
- The Supreme Court said that parts of it were unconstitutional and made Roosevelt stop them.
- It did very little that actually helped women and Native Americans.
- Most of the aid for farmers went to big farms, not small ones.

## 22. Popular culture in the 1930s

For example, three from:
- The government funded the WPA to employ writers, artists and actors. As well as giving these people jobs, the WPA meant that more people had access to the arts than before, and increased knowledge of American culture.
- People started to use cinema as a way to escape their troubles, so comedy, fantasy and musical films became popular.
- The experiences of the Depression inspired authors like John Steinbeck and Henry Roth to write some of the most famous books in American literature.
- Comic books were easily affordable and cheerful and became very popular in the late 1930s, especially with young people.
- Fewer people could afford to go to sports games, but more people began to play sports themselves, as they had more time.
- Radio became more popular as it allowed people to listen to music and follow sports without having to buy tickets.

## 23. Economic recovery

Any three from:
- After the neutrality laws were changed, America was able to export weapons to Britain and France. This created jobs in manufacturing and created income for the economy.
- Lend Lease increased demand for weapons and, as a result, manufacturing jobs.
- American rearmament meant millions were employed making planes, tanks and ships.
- Thousands joined the armed forces during rearmament and once America had joined the war after Pearl Harbor.
- Farmers had struggled during the Depression, but they were now needed to provide food for the army.

## 24. Social developments

One from the following:
- The employment opportunities for women increased their financial independence, and their involvement in the workplace and public life made them more engaged in politics.
- The important military contributions made by African Americans helped end segregation in the military and the FEPC fought for more equal treatment for African Americans in the workplace.

# Post-war America

## 25. Consumerism and prosperity

Any three from:
- The 1944 GI Bill was set up to support veterans with housing and education and helped people to learn skills that helped them into better paid and more stable employment.
- The Fair Deal (1945–53) improved housing and increased the minimum wage, which meant more income for workers on the lowest wages.
- Military spending continued during the Korean War, which boosted industries such as steel, chemicals, and electronics.
- President Eisenhower's focus on business meant that more businessmen were brought into the government to help boost the economy further.

## 26. The American Dream

Disagree (American Dream was real), any two from:
- America was more prosperous than ever, with booming manufacturing and high levels of exports.
- Employment was high and the minimum wage was increased, so people could afford a better standard of living.
- Efficient manufacturing methods developed during the war meant that more houses, cars, and domestic appliances could be produced, and that more people could afford them.

Agree (American Dream was a myth), any two from:
- A quarter of the population was living in poverty, which means that the American Dream was not a reality for everyone.
- The idea of the American Dream relied on each person being able to work hard and achieve success. However it ignored the discrimination against social groups like women and African Americans, which made it much more difficult for them to improve their circumstances.
- Republicans blocking Truman's attempts to introduce healthcare provision meant that not everyone could afford medical treatment, meaning the American Dream was likely to be out of their reach.

## 27. McCarthyism

Any three from:
- The communist USSR became a rival to America and began developing its own nuclear weapons.
- Communism spread across China and Eastern Europe and managing its spread through containment seemed to be failing.
- The Korean War between South Korea (supported by America) and North Korea (supported by the USSR) was going badly.
- Many accusations of spying and communist sympathies were made against government employees and influential people.

## 28. The Rock and Roll generation

Any three from:
- Teenagers had more time and money, so popular culture developed around the rebellious ways they dressed, spoke and behaved.
- Rock and roll music developed, showing a world where teenagers danced, drank and did other things that their parents didn't approve of.
- More houses had television sets, showing people 'ideal' families they were meant to aspire to.

- Products were developed alongside popular culture, giving people a way to spend money and become more like the people they saw on TV and in the movies.

## 29. Segregation and civil rights

Any four from:
- Segregation meant that African Americans could not use the same services as white people, such as public places, schools, drinking fountains and public transportation.
- Discrimination meant unequal access to housing and education, voting restrictions, and discrimination in work.
- Some African-American students such as Linda Brown had to travel much further to attend segregated schools, rather than the ones closest to them.
- African Americans such as Emmett Till faced violent discrimination and even death. Emmett Till's killers were allowed to go free.
- Even when African-American students were allowed into desegregated schools, they continued to face hostility and abuse.

## 30. Peaceful protest 1

Causes, any two from:
- After Brown vs Topeka, schools were desegregated and civil rights activists fought for public transport to be desegregated too.
- The murder of Emmett Till caused Rosa Parks to refuse to give up her seat, leading to her arrest.
- Martin Luther King's belief in peaceful direct action and his election to the MIA led to a non-violent boycott of the bus company.

Effects, any two from:
- The boycott gained public attention, and Martin Luther King's speeches and interviews meant that more people were aware of the discrimination against African Americans.
- Violence against protestors and civil rights activists increased, such as the bombing of Martin Luther King's house in 1956.
- Because of the boycott, the Supreme Court ruled that buses should no longer be segregated.

## 31. Peaceful protest 2

Any four from:
- African Americans would enter segregated or 'whites only' areas, showing their desire to be treated equally.
- Sit-ins were used as a non-violent method of resistance, such as in Greensboro.
- Freedom Riders travelled across the country to show that bus stations were still segregated, and African Americans still suffered from violence and harassment when using public transport.
- Peaceful marches took place in Birmingham, Washington, and Selma against the civil and economic discrimination encountered by African Americans.
- Volunteers tried to get as many African-American voters to register as possible, despite violent resistance.

## 32. Malcom X and Black Power

The non-violent protests encouraged by Martin Luther King were seen to be taking too long and not getting enough results. African Americans continued to be treated poorly and face discrimination, while the Civil Rights Acts of 1964 and 1968 convinced many white Americans that the fight for civil rights was over. The assassination of Martin Luther King led others to abandon non-violence.

## 33. Kennedy's social policies

Success, any three from:
- Gave more jobs to African Americans and challenged the discrimination that they faced.
- Cut taxes for the poorest people, increased the minimum wage, and improved social security.
- Improved roads, funded research and development in poor areas.
- Established the Peace Corps and helped young people to travel and learn.

Failure, any three from:
- Did not pass the Civil Rights Act in his lifetime, and only protected some African-American workers from discrimination.
- Provided funding that companies used to buy better equipment, putting more people out of work. Many still did not have jobs.
- Did nothing to help the poorest people take out loans to improve their houses, and could not pass legislation to give healthcare to the elderly.
- Did not pass his plans to provide federal funding for schools.

## 34. Johnson and the 'Great Society'

Kennedy, one from:
- Understood that America was facing huge changes, and came up with ideas to make the country a better place.
- Challenged discrimination against African Americans, and tried to make sure that the government didn't discriminate.

Johnson, one from:
- Was more successful in improving the lives of poor Americans through his housing, education, health and economic policies.
- Was able to pass much more legislation before the end of his presidency.

## 35. Feminist movements

Any two from:
- Feminism helped build the political pressure that passed the Equal Pay Act, ensuring that women had the right to equal pay to men for equal work.
- The Roe vs Wade case had an enormous impact on women, giving them the legal right to abortion. This gave women the power to decide what happened to their own bodies.
- Less discrimination and better employment opportunities meant that more women could pursue fulfilling careers and were no longer so obliged to stay at home.

# PRACTICE

## 46. Practice

1 Interpretations A and B both discuss the tactics used by African Americans in the campaign for civil rights in America. However, they offer different views about the effectiveness of non-violence. Seale – one of the founders of the Black Panther movement – claims that non-violent action didn't work because the protestors were powerless to stop themselves being 'pushed … into the corner' and the only way to escape was to fight back. On the other hand, Simkins argues that the non-violence advocated by King, using measures such as civil disobedience and economic boycotts, was a 'major factor' in the success of the movement.

## 47. Practice

2 Interpretations A and B offer different views about the effectiveness of non-violence in the campaign for civil rights in America because the writers come from different positions – Seale is explaining his own beliefs while Simkins is taking an overview of the whole movement. The interpretations also have a different purpose. In Interpretation B, Chris Simkins is a journalist telling the story of the civil rights movement and explaining the importance of Martin Luther King. King's insistence on non-violence was a key part of his campaigning. This was probably because non-violent protest was important in gaining support from the white population who saw peaceful protestors being attacked. He argues that non-violence was the main reason for his success. In Interpretation A, however, Bobby Seale of the Black Panther organisation is explaining that some African Americans were dissatisfied with a non-violent approach. He argues that demonstrating peacefully led to campaigners being attacked and was unsuccessful. He says that organisations like the Black Panthers developed because some African Americans felt that fighting back was their only option.

## 48. Practice

3 Either interpretation could be found more convincing.
- **To support Interpretation A:** I find Interpretation A more convincing because Bobby Seale was there at the time and is talking about why African Americans like him wanted to seek alternatives to the methods of Martin Luther King. First hand accounts like this are convincing because they tell us exactly how people at the time thought and felt, unlike Interpretation B, which was written after the time by someone trying to get an overview. Seale refers to the non-violent protestors being 'brutalized', and one of the main concerns of the Black Panther movement was that the police did little to protect African Americans from racist violence. Another concern of the movement was that the police were guilty of violence towards black Americans themselves. The Black Panthers ran armed patrols to check up on the police, so this interpretation fits with the historical context. Seale is pointing out that peaceful protestors who were acting lawfully had their impact reduced because the state did not protect them from racists. This convincingly explains why some African Americans chose more direct means.
- **To support Interpretation B:** I find Interpretation B more convincing because the author is a journalist who is taking a less biased view of the period, rather than defending his actions as Bobby Seale is doing in Interpretation A. Simkins points out that non-violence was a key part of Martin Luther King's approach and argues that it was a major factor in the success of the civil rights movement. This is persuasive as King wanted to make sure that African Americans were respected for obeying the law and being peaceful. It also fits with what we know about the period because the American public were horrified by police brutality towards peaceful protestors, such as the response to protests at Birmingham, Alabama. This encouraged public support for the civil rights movement.

## 50. Practice

4 Any two from the following:
- Growing tensions connected with increased immigration from eastern and southern Europe, including prejudice against immigrants and lack of integration.
- Segregation and the discrimination and violence faced by African Americans under Jim Crow laws.
- Social problems, such as alcohol poisoning and addiction, caused by prohibition.
- The rise of organised crime and the impact of mob violence and the corruption of police and public officials.

## 51. Practice

5 Answers could include the following:
- When America joined the First World War in 1917, men left to fight and women took over the jobs that they left behind. This helped to give these women some financial independence, and as a result more women took paid work after the war than they had done before America joined the fight.
- Financial independence meant that women had more options. The divorce rate doubled in the 1920s as women realised that they did not have to stay in unhappy marriages. More women chose to live on their own.
- As women had more opportunities, the restricting rules of 'proper' behaviour began to fall away. Many young women began to wear more revealing clothes, to smoke and drink – which were thought of as male habits at the time – and to stay out late. These women were known as flappers.
- Most changes affected upper and middle class women. For the majority of women life didn't change very much.

## 53. Practice

6 Either can be argued to be the more important reason.

For **social change**, answers could include:
- Abolishing prohibition was popular because it reduced the power of organised crime and created jobs. It also had an economic impact because the government raised money via taxation on alcohol.
- The National Recovery Administration – and later the 1935 Wagner Act – improved workers' rights and working conditions.
- The Works Progress Administration supported artists of all kinds to work through the Depression. These artistic works made many Americans more knowledgeable about their history and more involved in culture.

For **economic policy**, answers could include:
- The 1932 Emergency Banking Act restored trust in banks and made $1 billion available as loans.
- The 1932 Economy Act made money available to pay for New Deal programmes.
- The AAA – through raising prices – and FCA – through loans – supported farmers, who had struggled during the Depression.
- Job creation schemes reduced unemployment and the Gross National Product of the country rose as a result.

Social change and economic policy are connected as many social problems, such as unemployment, had economic solutions – such as schemes like the CCC and CWA – so economic measures had a social impact and vice versa.

# Notes

# Notes

Published by Pearson Education Limited, 80 Strand, London, WC2R 0RL.

www.pearsonschoolsandfecolleges.co.uk

Text and illustrations © Pearson Education Ltd 2018
Produced by Just Content Ltd, Braintree, Essex
Typeset by PDQ Digital Media Solutions Ltd, Bungay, Suffolk
Cover illustration by Eoin Coveney

The right of Sally Clifford to be identified as author of this work has been asserted by her in accordance with the Copyright, Designs and Patents Act 1988.

First published 2018

24
10 9 8 7 6 5

**British Library Cataloguing in Publication Data**
A catalogue record for this book is available from the British Library

ISBN 978 1 292 24291 0

Printed and bound in Great Britain by Bell and Bain Ltd, Glasgow

**Acknowledgements**
Content written by Rob Bircher, Brian Dowse, Victoria Payne and Kirsty Taylor is included.

**Text:**
**p38: SB Fuller and Joe L Dudley Sr. Foundation Inc:** Fuller, SB. Washington Post, 1980. https://www.washingtonpost.com/archive/opinions/1980/09/21/sb-fuller/99178e22-48f1-4700-b664-c98726d4b792/?utm_term=.9c432ad6308b;
**p45: VOA news:** Simkins. Non-violence Was Key to Civil Rights Movement, 2014. https://www.voanews.com/a/nonviolencekey-to-civil-rights-movement/1737280.html

**Pearson acknowledges use of the following extracts**
**p38: Oxford University Press:** Kennedy, David M. The American People in the Great Depression: Freedom from Fear, Part One. Oxford University Press, 2003; **p45: Washington University in St. Louis:** Interview with Bobby Seale. Washington University Libraries, Film and Media Archive, Henry Hampton Collection. 1988. http://digital.wustl.edu/e/eii/eiiweb/sea5427.0172.147bobbyseale.html

The author and publisher would like to thank the following individuals and organisations for permission to reproduce photographs:

(Key: t-top; b-bottom; c-centre; l-left; r-right; tr-top right; cl-centre left; cr-centre right)

**Alamy Stock photo:** Archive Pics 3tr, Pictorial Press Ltd 3cr; Granger-Historical Picture Archive 7cl, 10, 20; H.Armstrong Roberts/Classicstock 7cr; Chronicle 15; GL Archive 17; IanDagnall Computing 18; Everett Collection Inc 24, 30; World History Archive 32; **Getty Images:** Hulton Archive/Archive Photos 28.